Shelf
Life

Alex Johnson

Shelf Life

*Writers on Books
and Reading*

First published 2018 by
The British Library
96 Euston Road
London NW1 2DB

Cataloguing in Publication Data
A catalogue record for this publication is available from
The British Library

ISBN 978 0 7123 5286 4

Typeset and cover by Sandra Friesen
Printed and bound by Gutenberg Press, Malta

For
Philip and Phyllis,
Wilma,
Thomas, Edward and Robert

❡

Contents

Introduction

We are surrounding ourselves with bookishness more than ever before. You can stay in library-themed hotels around the world, slouch on armchairs with built-in bookshelves at home, and run your own Airbnb bookshop in Scotland for a week. And it's not just books, an entire literary lifestyle is now available on demand. Decorate your sitting room with bookcase wallpaper. Slice your carrots on Romeo and Julienne chopping boards. Spray yourself with "Mr Darcy" fragrance. Apply temporary literary tattoos ("I declare after all there is no enjoyment like reading!"). Buy a shower curtain that looks like Bilbo's front door.

But while we have developed the technology to carry an entire library almost weightlessly in our handbags, the delights of bibliomania are nothing new—the writings we have brought together in the collection you have in your hands feature the thoughts of some of the giants of world literature on the subject of books and reading over the last 400 years.

Our interest in books about books and writers on writing is insatiable and many readers will be familiar with Orwell on bookselling, Woolf on how to read, and Eco on the end of the book. The musings on the following pages take us by the hand and show us behind the scenes of the written word. They reveal the nuts and bolts of books in the same way that daily transfer gossip supplements the diet of football fans or that the extras on the making of the film on DVDs satisfy film buffs.

So prepare yourself to hear from an iconic Prime Minister about the best way to store your books and from an illustrious US President about what to read outdoors. Then enjoy serious speculations on the psychological implications of reading from a 19th century philosopher, and less serious ones concerning the problems of getting rid of unwanted volumes from one of the world's most famous literary cricketers. These essays and commentaries—and indeed one or two of the writers—have been largely and unjustly forgotten, but they are certainly not past their sell-by date, and deserve the longest possible shelf life.

Alex Johnson is a journalist, blogger and the author of A Book of Book Lists *published by The British Library as well as* Improbable Libraries, Bookshelf, *and* Shedworking: The Alternative Workplace Revolution. *He runs the websites Shedworking (www.shedworking.co.uk), Bookshelf (www. onthebookshelf.co.uk) and the micro life (www.themicrolife. co.uk). Alex lives in St Albans with his wife, three children, and several shelves of books about books.*

Boys, however, are by far more destructive than girls ❡

The Enemies of Books

William Blades

Books are fragile. In his 1880 lengthy list of dangers to their survival, 19th century printer, writer and book collector William Blades warns strenuously and in considerable detail about fire, water, gas, heat—including using books to bake pies—dust, neglect, ignorance, bookworms, other vermin, bookbinders, collectors and servants. The excerpt below covers his thoughts about the threat that children pose as potential "biblioclasts" or book destroyers. "The possession of any old book is a sacred trust," he writes, "which a conscientious owner or guardian would as soon think of ignoring as a parent would of neglecting his child." The section on bookworms is especially intriguing as Blades recounts how a bookbinder from Northampton sent him a fat one which he kept alive for three weeks, feeding it tiny pieces of Boethius's The Consolation of

Philosophy *from a book produced by William Caxton until it perished ("either from too much fresh air, from unaccustomed liberty, or from change of food"). Indeed, in addition to his interest in bibliodamage, Blades analysed the works of the famous printer in his book* Life and Typography of William Caxton, England's First Printer *(1861–63). After his death in 1890, his impressive private library was bought by the St Bride Foundation cultural centre in London which used it to help establish its own library.*

Children, with all their innocence, are often guilty of book-murder. I must confess to having once taken down Humphreys' *History of Writing*, which contains many brightly-coloured plates, to amuse a sick daughter. The object was certainly gained, but the consequences of so bad a precedent were disastrous. That copy (which, I am glad to say, was easily re-placed), notwithstanding great care on my part, became soiled and torn, and at last was given up to Nursery martyrdom. Can I regret it? surely not, for, although bibliographically sinful, who can weigh the amount of real pleasure received, and actual pain ignored, by the patient in the contemplation of those beautifully-blended colours?

A neighbour of mine some few years ago suffered severely from a propensity, apparently irresistible, in one of his daughters to tear his library books. She was six years old, and would go quietly to a shelf and take down a book or two, and having torn a dozen leaves or so down the middle, would replace the volumes, fragments and all, in their places, the damage being undiscovered until the books were wanted for use. Reprimand, expostulation and even punishment were of no avail; but a single "whipping" effected a cure.

Boys, however, are by far more destructive than girls, and have, naturally, no reverence for age, whether in man or books. Who does not fear a schoolboy with his first pocket-knife? As Wordsworth did not say:—

"You may trace him oft
 By scars which his activity has left
 Upon our shelves and volumes....
 He who with pocket-knife will cut the edge
 Of luckless panel or of prominent book,
 Detaching with a stroke a label here, a
  back-band there."

Excursion III, 83.

Pleased, too, are they, if, with mouths full of candy, and sticky fingers, they can pull in and out the books on your bottom shelves, little knowing the damage and pain they will cause. One would fain cry out, calling on the Shade of Horace to pardon the false quantity—

"Magna movet stomacho fastidia, si puer unctis
 Tractavit volumen manibus."[1]

Sat. IV.

1 "It moves the stomach to great disgust, if a boy treats volumes with oily hands"

What boys *can* do may be gathered from the following true story, sent me by a correspondent who was the immediate sufferer:—

One summer day he met in town an acquaintance who for many years had been abroad; and finding his appetite for old books as keen as ever, invited him home to have a mental feed upon "fifteeners" and other bibliographical dainties, preliminary to the coarser pleasures enjoyed at the dinner-table. The "home" was an old mansion in the outskirts of London, whose very architecture was suggestive of black-letter and sheep-skin. The weather, alas! was rainy, and, as they approached the house, loud peals of laughter reached their ears. The children were keeping a birthday with a few young friends. The damp forbad all outdoor play, and, having been left too much to their own devices, they had invaded the library. It was just after the Battle of Balaclava, and the heroism of the combatants on that hard-fought field was in everybody's mouth. So the mischievous young imps divided themselves into two opposing camps—Britons and Russians. The Russian division was just inside the door, behind ramparts formed of old folios and quartos taken from the bottom shelves and piled to the height of about four feet. It was a wall of old fathers, fifteenth century chronicles, county histories, Chaucer, Lydgate, and such like.

Some few yards off were the Britishers, provided with heaps of small books as missiles, with which they kept up a skirmishing cannonade against the foe. Imagine the tableau! Two elderly gentlemen enter hurriedly, pater-familias receiving, quite unintentionally, the first edition of *Paradise Lost* in the pit of his stomach, his friend nar-rowly escaping a closer personal acquaintance with a quarto *Hamlet* than he had ever had before. Finale: great outburst of wrath, and rapid retreat of the combatants, many wounded (volumes) being left on the field.

Every passion borders on the chaotic ❡

Unpacking My Library

Walter Benjamin

*Many readers are also collectors and cultural critic and Ger-
man man of letters Walter Benjamin (1892–1940) takes this
as the subject for his charming essay, "Unpacking My Library:
A Talk about Book Collecting" (1931). His central focus is the
relationship between people and their books, the pleasure in
rediscovering forgotten titles after two years of separation from
his books, and how they provide madeleine moment links to
people, places and events. Without giving any kind of a list of
what he's actually unpacking (at the end of the essay he still
has half a box to get through), Benjamin examines the act of
acquiring books—by writing, borrowing or buying them—the
importance of their former ownership, the craftsmanship of
book production, and the emotions books provide. Even though
many people never reread the books in their library, this all*

adds up to what he sees as a "magic encyclopaedia", a collection which tells the individual's life story. Much of the rest of Benjamin's work focuses on art and literature and his earlier essay "The Task of the Translator" (1921) reflects his interest in translation as an art form (he translated Baudelaire and Proust). He committed suicide in 1940 while on the run from the Nazis.

I am unpacking my library. Yes, I am. The books are not yet on the shelves, not yet touched by the mild boredom of order. I cannot march up and down their ranks to pass them in review before a friendly audience. You need not fear any of that. Instead, I must ask you to join me in the disorder of crates that have been wrenched open, the air saturated with the dust of wood, the floor covered with torn paper, to join me among piles of volumes that are seeing daylight again after two years of darkness, so that you may be ready to share with me a bit of the mood—it is certainly not an elegiac mood but, rather, one of anticipation—which these books arouse in a genuine collector. For such a man is speaking to you, and on closer scrutiny he proves to be speaking only about himself. Would it not be presumptuous of me if, in order to appear convincingly objective and down-to-earth, I enumerated for you the main sections or prize pieces of a library, if I presented you with their history or even their usefulness to a writer? I, for one, have in mind something less obscure, something more palpable than that; what I am really concerned with is giving you some insight into the relationship of a book collector to his possessions, into collecting rather than a collection. If I do this by elaborating on the various ways of acquiring books, this is something entirely arbitrary. This or any other procedure is merely a dam against the spring tide of memories which surges toward any collector as he contemplates his possessions. Every passion borders on the chaotic, but the collector's passion borders on the chaos of memories. More than that: the chance, the fate, that suffuse the past before my eyes are conspicuously present in the accustomed confusion of these books. For what else is this collection but a disorder to which habit has accommodated itself to such an extent that it can appear as order? You have all heard of people whom the loss of their books has turned into invalids, or of those who in order to acquire them became criminals. These are the very areas in which any order is a balancing act of extreme precariousness. "The only exact knowledge there is," said Anatole France, "is the knowledge of the date of publication and the format of books." And indeed, if there is a counterpart to the confusion of a library, it is the order of its catalogue.

Thus there is in the life of a collector a dialectical tension between the poles of disorder and order. Naturally, his existence is tied to many other things as well: to a very mysterious relationship to ownership, something about which we shall have more to say later; also, to a relationship to objects which does not emphasize their functional, utilitarian value—that is, their usefulness—but studies and loves them as the scene, the stage, of their fate. The most profound enchantment for the collector is the locking of individual items within a magic circle in which they are fixed as the final thrill, the thrill of acquisition, passes over them. Everything remembered and thought, everything conscious, becomes the pedestal, the frame, the base, the lock of his property. The period, the region, the craftsmanship, the former ownership—for a true collector the whole background of an item adds up to a magic encyclopaedia whose quintessence is the fate of his object. In this circumscribed area, then, it may be surmised how the great physiognomists—and collectors are the physiognomists of the world of objects—turn into interpreters of fate. One has only to watch a collector handle the objects in his glass case. As he holds them in his hands, he seems to be seeing through them into their distant past as though inspired. So much for the magical side of the collector—his old-age image, I might call it.

Habent sua fata libelli[1]: these words may have been intended as a general statement about books. So books like *The Divine Comedy*, Spinoza's *Ethics*, and *The Origin of Species* have their fates. A collector, however, interprets this Latin saying differently. For him, not only books but

1 "Books have their own destiny"—part of the full phrase *Pro captu lectoris habent sua fata libelli*, which states that the destiny of the books is in accordance with the capability of the reader.

15

also copies of books have their fates. And in this sense, the most important fate of a copy is its encounter with him, with his own collection. I am not exaggerating when I say that to a true collector the acquisition of an old book is its rebirth. This is the childlike element which in a collector mingles with the element of old age. For children can accomplish the renewal of existence in a hundred unfailing ways. Among children, collecting is only one process of renewal; other processes are the painting of objects, the cutting out of figures, the application of decals—the whole range of childlike modes of acquisition, from touching things to giving them names. To renew the old world—that is the collector's deepest desire when he is driven to acquire new things, and that is why a collector of older books is closer to the wellsprings of collecting than the acquirer of luxury editions. How do books cross the threshold of a collection and become the property of a collector? The history of their acquisition is the subject of the following remarks.

Of all the ways of acquiring books, writing them oneself is regarded as the most praiseworthy method. At this point many of you will remember with pleasure the large library which Jean Paul's poor little schoolmaster Wutz gradually acquired by writing, himself, all the works whose titles interested him in book-fair catalogues; after all, he could not afford to buy them. Writers are really people who write books not because they are poor, but because they are dissatisfied with the books which they could buy but do not like. You, ladies and gentlemen, may regard this as a whimsical definition of a writer. But everything said from the angle of a real collector is whimsical. Of the customary modes of acquisition, the one most appropriate to a collector would be the borrowing of a book with its attendant non-returning. The book borrower of real stature whom we envisage here proves himself to be an inveterate collector of books not so much by the fervour with which he guards his borrowed treasures and by the deaf ear which he turns to all reminders from the everyday world of legality as by his failure to read these books. If my experience may serve as evidence, a man is more likely to return a borrowed book upon occasion than to read it. And the non-reading of books, you will object, should be characteristic of collectors? This is news to me, you may say. It is not news at all. Experts will bear me out when I say that it is the oldest thing in the world. Suffice it to quote the answer which Anatole France gave to a philistine who admired his library and then finished with the standard question, "And you have read all these books, Monsieur France?" "Not one-tenth of them. I don't suppose you use your Sèvres china every day?"

Incidentally, I have put the right to such an attitude to the test. For years, for at least the first third of its existence, my library consisted of no more than two or three shelves which increased only by inches each year. This was its militant age, when no book was allowed to enter it without the certification that I had not read it. Thus I might never have acquired a library extensive enough to be worthy of the name if there had not been an inflation. Suddenly the emphasis shifted; books acquired real value, or, at any rate, were difficult to obtain. At least this is how it seemed in Switzerland. At the eleventh hour I sent my first major book orders from there and in this way was able to secure such irreplaceable items as *Der blaue Reiter* and Bachofen's *Sage von Tanaquil*, which could still be obtained from the publishers at that time.

Well—so you may say—after exploring all these byways we should finally reach the wide highway of book acquisition, namely, the purchasing of books. This is indeed a wide highway, but not a comfortable one. The purchasing done by a book collector has very little in common with that done in a bookshop by a student getting a textbook, a man of the world buying a present for his lady, or a businessman intending to while away his next train journey. I have made my most memorable purchases on trips, as a transient. Property and possession belong to the tactical sphere. Collectors are people with a tactical instinct; their experience teaches them that when they capture a strange city, the smallest antique shop can be a fortress, the most remote stationery store a key position. How many cities have revealed themselves to me in the marches I undertook in the pursuit of books!

By no means all of the most important purchases are made on the premises of a dealer. Catalogues play a far greater part. And even though the purchaser may be thoroughly acquainted with the book ordered from a catalogue, the individual copy always remains a surprise and the order always a bit of a gamble. There are grievous disappointments, but also happy finds. I remember, for instance, that I once ordered a book with coloured illustrations for my old collection of children's books only because it contained fairy tales by Albert Ludwig Grimm and was published at Grimma, Thuringia. Grimma was also the place of publication of a book of fables edited by the same Albert Ludwig Grimm. With its sixteen illustrations my copy of this book of fables was the only extant example of the early work of the great German book illustrator Lyser, who lived in Hamburg around the middle of the last century. Well, my reaction to the consonance of the names had been correct. In this case too I discovered the work of Lyser, namely *Lina's Märchenbuch*, a work which has remained unknown to his bibliographers and which deserves a more detailed reference than this first one I am introducing here.

The acquisition of books is by no means a matter of money or expert knowledge alone. Not even both factors together suffice for the establishment of a real library, which is always somewhat impenetrable and at the same time uniquely itself. Anyone who buys from catalogues must have flair in addition to the qualities I have mentioned. Dates, place names, formats, previous owners, bindings, and the like: all these details must tell him something—not as dry, isolated facts, but as a harmonious whole; from the quality and intensity of this harmony he must be able to recognize whether a book is for him or not. An auction requires yet another set of qualities in a collector. To the reader of a catalogue the book itself must speak, or possibly its previous ownership if the provenance of the copy has been established. A man who wishes to participate at an auction must pay equal attention to the book and to his competitors, in addition to keeping a cool enough head to avoid being carried away in the competition. It is a frequent occurrence that someone gets stuck with a high purchase price because he kept raising his bid—more to assert himself than to acquire the book. On the other hand, one of the finest memories of a collector is the moment when he rescued a book to which he might never have given a thought, much less a wishful look, because he found it lonely and abandoned on the market place and bought it to give it its freedom the way the prince bought a beautiful slave girl in *The Arabian Nights*. To a book collector, you see, the true freedom of all books is somewhere on his shelves.

To this day, Balzac's *La Peau de chagrin* stands out from long rows of French volumes in my library as a memento of my most exciting experience at an auction. This happened in 1915 at the Rumann auction put up by Emil Hirsch, one of the greatest of book experts and most distinguished of dealers. The edition in question appeared in 1838 in Paris, Place de la Bourse. As I pick up my copy, I see not only its number in the Rumann collection, but even the label of the shop in which the first owner bought the book over ninety years ago for one eightieth of today's price. "Papeterie I. Flanneau," it says. A fine age in which it was still possible to buy such a de luxe edition at a stationery dealer's! The steel engravings of this book were designed by the foremost French graphic artist and executed by the foremost engravers. But I was going to tell you how I acquired this book. I had gone to Emil Hirsch's for an advance inspection and had handled forty or fifty volumes; that particular volume had inspired in me the ardent desire to hold on to it forever. The day of the auction came. As chance would have it, in the sequence of the auction this copy of *La Peau de chagrin* was preceded by a complete set of its illustrations printed separately on India paper. The bidders sat at a long table; diagonally across from me sat the man who was the focus of all eyes at the first bid, the famous Munich collector Baron von Simolin. He was greatly interested in this set, but he had rival bidders; in short, there was a spirited contest which resulted in the highest bid of the entire auction—far in excess of three thousand marks. No one seemed to have expected such a high figure, and all those present were quite excited. Emil Hirsch remained unconcerned, and whether he wanted to save time or was guided by some other consideration, he proceeded to the next item, with no one really paying attention. He called out the price, and with my heart pounding and with the full realization that I was unable to compete with any of those big collectors I bid a somewhat higher amount. Without arousing the bidders' attention, the auctioneer went through the usual routine—"Do I hear more?" and three bangs of his gavel, with an eternity seeming to separate each from the next—and proceeded to add the auctioneer's charge. For a student like me the sum was still considerable. The following morning at the pawnshop is no longer part of this story, and I prefer to speak about another incident which I should like to call the negative of an auction. It happened last year at a Berlin auction. The collection of books that was offered was a miscellany in quality and subject matter, and only a number of rare works on occultism and natural philosophy were worthy of note. I bid for a number of them, but each time I noticed a gentleman in the front row who seemed only to have waited for my bid to counter with his own, evidently prepared to top any offer. After this had been repeated several times, I gave up all hope of acquiring the book which I was most interested in that day. It was the rare *Fragmente aus dem Nachlass eines jungen Physikers* [Posthumous Fragments of a Young Physicist] which Johann Wilhelm Ritter published in two volumes at Heidelberg in 1810. This work has never been reprinted, but I have always considered its preface, in which the author-editor tells the story of his life in the guise of an obituary for his supposedly deceased unnamed friend—with whom he is really identical—as the most important sample of personal prose of German Romanticism. Just as the item came up I had a brain wave. It was simple enough: since my bid was bound to give the item to the other man, I must not bid at all. I controlled myself and remained silent. What I had hoped for came about: no interest, no bid, and the book was put aside. I deemed it wise to let several days go by, and when I appeared on the premises after a week, I found the book in the secondhand department and benefited by the lack of interest when I acquired it.

Once you have approached the mountains of cases in order to mine the books from them and bring them to the light of day—or, rather, of night—what memories crowd in upon you! Nothing highlights the fascination of unpacking more clearly than the difficulty of stopping this activity. I had started at noon, and it was midnight before I had worked my way to the last cases. Now I put my hands on two volumes bound in faded boards which, strictly speaking, do not belong in a book case at all: two albums with stick-in pictures which my mother pasted in as a child and which I inherited. They are the seeds of a collection of children's books which is growing steadily even today, though no longer in my garden. There is no living library that does not harbour a number of book-like creations from fringe areas. They need not be stick-in albums or family albums, autograph books or portfolios containing pamphlets or religious tracts; some people become attached to leaflets and prospectuses, others to handwriting facsimiles or typewritten copies of unobtainable books; and certainly periodicals can form the prismatic fringes of a library. But to get back to those albums: Actually, inheritance is the soundest way of acquiring a collection. For a collector's attitude toward his possessions stems from an owner's feeling of responsibility toward his property. Thus it is, in the highest sense, the attitude of an heir, and the most distinguished trait of a collection will always be its transmissibility. You should know that in saying this I fully realize that my discussion of the mental climate of collecting will confirm many of you in your conviction that this passion is behind the times, in your distrust of the collector type. Nothing is further from my mind than to shake either your conviction or your distrust. But one thing should be noted: the phenomenon of collecting loses its meaning as it loses its personal owner. Even though public collections may be less objectionable socially and more useful academically than private collections, the objects get their due only in the latter. I do know that time is running out for the type that I am discussing here and have been representing before you a bit *ex officio*. But, as Hegel put it, only when it is dark does the owl of Minerva begin its flight. Only in extinction is the collector comprehended.

Now I am on the last half-emptied case and it is way past midnight. Other thoughts fill me than the ones I am talking about—not thoughts but images, memories. Memories of the cities in which I found so many things: Riga, Naples, Munich, Danzig, Moscow, Florence, Basel, Paris; memories of Rosenthal's sumptuous rooms in Munich, of the Danzig Stockturm where the late Hans Rhaue was domiciled, of Süssengut's musty book cellar in North Berlin; memories of the rooms where these books had been housed, of my student's den in Munich, of my room in Bern, of the solitude of Iseltwald on the Lake of Brienz, and finally of my boyhood room, the former location of only four or five of the several thousand volumes that are piled up around me. O bliss of the collector, bliss of the man of leisure! Of no one has less been expected, and no one has had a greater sense of wellbeing than the man who has been able to carry on his disreputable existence in the mask of Spitzweg's "Bookworm." For inside him there are spirits, or at least little genii, which have seen to it that for a collector—and I mean a real collector, a collector as he ought to be—ownership is the most intimate relationship that one can have to objects. Not that they come alive in him; it is he who lives in them. So I have erected one of his dwellings, with books as the building stones, before you, and now he is going to disappear inside, as is only fitting.

That girl hasn't waited fifty pages for nothing ⁊

A Lesson in Fiction

Stephen Leacock

One hundred years ago, Stephen Leacock (1869–1944) was probably the most famous humorist writing in English in the world. Born in the village of Swanmoor near Southampton, his family emigrated to Canada when he was 6. Although he became Professor of Political Economy at McGill University and wrote the standard textbook Elements of Political Science *(1906), he was better known as the writer of light parody and satire in collections of his short writings such as* Literary Lapses *(1910—in which "A Lesson in Fiction", below, appears) and particularly* Sunshine Sketches of a Little Town *(1912), a forerunner of* Garrison Keillor's Lake Wobegon. *These works made him a household name and he undertook many lecture tours, including a mammoth one to England and Scotland in 1921.*

Leacock inspired many comedians and writers—F Scott Fitzgerald wrote him a fan letter, Spike Milligan was a huge admirer, and the one-downmanship of the "Four Yorkshiremen" sketch from At Last the 1948 Show *and* Monty Python *owes much to Leacock's "Self Made Men" piece. A short animation of perhaps his most famous essay— "My Financial Career"—was nominated for an Oscar in 1964. He is also one of the many people to whom variations on the saying "I am a* great believer in luck *and I find the harder I work the more I have of it" is attributed. The Stephen Leacock Memorial Medal has been awarded annually since 1947 for the best book of humour written in English by a Canadian writer.*

Suppose that in the opening pages of the modern melodramatic novel you find some such situation as the following, in which is depicted the terrific combat between Gaspard de Vaux, the boy lieutenant, and Hairy Hank, the chief of the Italian banditti:

"The inequality of the contest was apparent. With a mingled yell of rage and contempt, his sword brandished above his head and his dirk between his teeth, the enormous bandit rushed upon his intrepid opponent. De Vaux seemed scarce more than a stripling, but he stood his ground and faced his hitherto invincible assailant. 'Mong Dieu,' cried De Smythe, 'he is lost!'"

Question. On which of the parties to the above contest do you honestly feel inclined to put your money?

Answer. On De Vaux. He'll win. Hairy Hank will force him down to one knee and with a brutal cry of "Har! har!" will be about to dirk him, when De Vaux will make a sudden lunge (one he had learnt at home out of a book of lunges) and—

Very good. You have answered correctly. Now, suppose you find, a little later in the book, that the killing of Hairy

Hank has compelled De Vaux to flee from his native land to the East. Are you not fearful for his safety in the desert?

Answer. Frankly, I am not. De Vaux is all right. His name is on the title page, and you can't kill him.

Question. Listen to this, then: "The sun of Ethiopia beat fiercely upon the desert as De Vaux, mounted upon his faithful elephant, pursued his lonely way. Seated in his lofty hoo-doo, his eye scoured the waste. Suddenly a solitary horseman appeared on the horizon, then another, and another, and then six. In a few moments a whole crowd of solitary horsemen swooped down upon him. There was a fierce shout of 'Allah!' a rattle of firearms. De Vaux sank from his hoo-doo on to the sands, while the affrighted elephant dashed off in all directions. The bullet had struck him in the heart."

There now, what do you think of that? Isn't De Vaux killed now?

Answer. I am sorry. De Vaux is not dead. True, the ball had hit him, oh yes, it had hit him, but it had glanced off against a family Bible, which he carried in his waistcoat in case of illness, struck some hymns that he had in his hip-pocket, and, glancing off again, had flattened itself against De Vaux's diary of his life in the desert, which was in his knapsack.

Question. But even if this doesn't kill him, you must admit that he is near death when he is bitten in the jungle by the deadly dongola?

Answer. That's all right. A kindly Arab will take De Vaux to the Sheik's tent.

Question. What will De Vaux remind the Sheik of?

Answer. Too easy. Of his long-lost son, who disappeared years ago.

Question. Was this son Hairy Hank?

Answer. Of course he was. Anyone could see that, but the Sheik never suspects it, and heals De Vaux. He heals him with an herb, a thing called a simple, an amazingly simple, known only to the Sheik. Since using this herb, the Sheik has used no other.

Question. The Sheik will recognize an overcoat that De Vaux is wearing, and complications will arise in the matter of Hairy Hank deceased. Will this result in the death of the boy lieutenant?

Answer. No. By this time De Vaux has realized that the reader knows he won't die and resolves to quit the desert. The thought of his mother keeps recurring to him, and of his father, too, the grey, stooping old man—does he stoop still or has he stopped stooping? At times, too, there comes the thought of another, a fairer than his father; she whose—but enough, De Vaux returns to the old homestead in Piccadilly.

Question. When De Vaux returns to England, what will happen?

Answer. This will happen: "He who left England ten years before a raw boy, has returned a sunburnt soldierly man. But who is this that advances smilingly to meet him? Can the mere girl, the bright child that shared his hours of play, can she have grown into this peerless, graceful girl, at whose feet half the noble suitors of England are kneeling? 'Can this be her?' he asks himself in amazement."

Question. Is it her?

Answer. Oh, it's her all right. It is her, and it is him, and it is them. That girl hasn't waited fifty pages for nothing.

Question. You evidently guess that a love affair will ensue between the boy lieutenant and the peerless girl with the broad feet. Do you imagine, however, that its course will run smoothly and leave nothing to record?

Answer. Not at all. I feel certain that the scene of the novel having edged itself around to London, the writer will not feel satisfied unless he introduces the following famous scene:

"Stunned by the cruel revelation which he had received, unconscious of whither his steps were taking him, Gaspard de Vaux wandered on in the darkness from street to street until he found himself upon London Bridge. He leaned over the parapet and looked down upon the whirling stream below. There was something in the still, swift rush of it that seemed to beckon, to allure him. After all, why not? What was life now that he should prize it? For a moment De Vaux paused irresolute."

Question. Will he throw himself in?

Answer. Well, say you don't know Gaspard. He will pause irresolute up to the limit, then, with a fierce struggle, will recall his courage and hasten from the Bridge.

Question. This struggle not to throw oneself in must be dreadfully difficult?

Answer. Oh! dreadfully! Most of us are so frail we should jump in at once. But Gaspard has the knack of it. Besides he still has some of the Sheik's herb; he chews it.

Question. What has happened to De Vaux anyway? Is it anything he has eaten?

Answer. No, it is nothing that he has eaten. It's about her. The blow has come. She has no use for sunburn, doesn't care for tan; she is going to marry a duke and the boy lieutenant is no longer in it. The real trouble is that the modern novelist has got beyond the happy-marriage mode of ending. He wants tragedy and a blighted life to wind up with.

Question. How will the book conclude?

Answer. Oh, De Vaux will go back to the desert, fall upon the Sheik's neck, and swear to be a second Hairy Hank to him. There will be a final panorama of the desert, the Sheik and his newly found son at the door of the tent, the sun setting behind a pyramid, and De Vaux's faithful elephant crouched at his feet and gazing up at him with dumb affection.

I should not care to be caught in the serious avenues of some cathedral alone, and reading Candide. ¶

Detached Thoughts on Books and Reading

Charles Lamb

It would be unthinkable in a book of essays about books not to include the work of Charles Lamb (1775–1834). Though sadly largely forgotten in the 21st century, Lamb is probably best known today for his Tales from Shakespeare *(1807) which he wrote with his troubled sister Mary, a collection of summaries aimed at children of the key comedies and tragedies. In his heyday though, he was a hugely popular essayist (and minor poet, his "The Old Familiar Faces" is often anthologized), writing especially for* The London Magazine *under the pseudonym "Elia". His pieces were collected in* Essays of Elia *(1823) and, 10 years later,* More Essays of Elia, *from which "Detached Thoughts on Books and Reading" below is taken. It asks many timeless questions about books, what they should look like, when and where they should be read, and* describes "books which are no books", what Lamb describes as "biblia a-biblia". Although he spent most of his working life as a clerk in the British East India Company, Lamb was close to the major literary figures of the day including William Wordsworth, Samuel Taylor Coleridge (a friend since school-days) and William Hazlitt, while he and Mary ran a popular literary salon at their London home.

To mind the inside of a book is to entertain one's self with the forced product of another man's brain. Now I think a man of quality and breeding may be much amused with the natural sprouts of his own."—Lord Foppington in *The Relapse*.

An ingenious acquaintance of my own was so much struck with this bright sally of his Lordship, that he has left off reading altogether, to the great improvement of his originality. At the hazard of losing some credit on this head, I must confess that I dedicate no inconsiderable portion of my time to other people's thoughts. I dream away my life in others' speculations. I love to lose myself in other men's minds. When I am not walking, I am reading, I cannot sit and think. Books think for me.

I have no repugnances. Shaftesbury is not too genteel for me, nor Jonathan Wild too low. I can read anything which I call a book. There are things in that shape which I cannot allow for such.

In this catalogue of "books which are no books"—"biblia a-biblia"—I reckon Court Calendars, Directories, Pocket Books, Draught Boards bound and lettered at the back, Scientific Treatises, Almanacks, Statutes at Large; the works of Hume, Gibbon, Robertson, Beattie, Soame Jenyns, and, generally, all those volumes which "no gentleman's library should be without:" the *Histories of Flavius*

Josephus (that learned Jew), and Paley's *Moral Philosophy*. With these exceptions, I can read almost anything. I bless my stars for a taste so catholic, so unexcluding.

I confess that it moves my spleen to see these things in books' clothing perched upon shelves, like false saints, usurpers of true shrines, intruders into the sanctuary, thrusting out the legitimate occupants. To reach down a well-bound semblance of a volume, and hope it is some kind-hearted play-book, then, opening what "seem its leaves," to come bolt upon a withering Population Essay. To expect a Steele, or a Farquhar, and find—Adam Smith. To view a well-arranged assortment of blockheaded Encyclopaedias (Anglicanas or Metropolitanas) set out in an array of Russia, or Morocco, when a tithe of that good leather would comfortably re-clothe my shivering folios; would renovate Paracelsus himself, and enable old Raymund Lully to look like himself again in the world. I never see these impostors, but I long to strip them, to warm my ragged veterans in their spoils.

To be strong-backed and neat-bound is the desideratum of a volume. Magnificence comes after. This, when it can be afforded, is not to be lavished upon all kinds of books indiscriminately. I would not dress a set of Magazines, for instance, in full suit. The dishabille, or half-binding (with Russia backs ever) is our costume.

A Shakspeare, or a Milton (unless the first editions), it were mere foppery to trick out in gay apparel. The possession of them confers no distinction. The exterior of them (the things themselves being so common), strange to say, raises no sweet emotions, no tickling sense of property in the owner. Thomson's *Seasons*, again, looks best (I maintain it) a little torn, and dog's-eared. How beautiful to a genuine lover of reading are the sullied leaves, and worn out appearance, nay, the very odour (beyond Russia), if we would not forget kind feelings in fastidiousness, of an old "Circulating Library" *Tom Jones*, or *Vicar of Wakefield*! How they speak of the thousand thumbs, that have turned over their pages with delight!—of the lone sempstress, whom they may have cheered (milliner, or harder-working mantua-maker) after her long day's needle-toil, running far into midnight, when she has snatched an hour, ill spared from sleep, to steep her cares, as in some Lethean cup, in spelling out their enchanting contents! Who would have them a whit less soiled? What better condition could we desire to see them in?

In some respects the better a book is, the less it demands from binding. Fielding, Smollet, Sterne, and all that class of perpetually self-reproductive volumes—Great Nature's Stereotypes—we see them individually perish with less regret, because we know the copies of them to be "eterne." But where a book is at once both good and rare—where the individual is almost the species, and when that perishes,

> We know not where is that Promethean torch
> That can its light relumine—

such a book, for instance, as the *Life of the Duke of Newcastle*, by his Duchess—no casket is rich enough, no casing sufficiently durable, to honour and keep safe such a jewel.

Not only rare volumes of this description, which seem hopeless ever to be reprinted; but old editions of writers, such as Sir Philip Sydney, Bishop Taylor, Milton in his prose-works, Fuller—of whom we have reprints, yet the books themselves, though they go about, and are talked of here and there, we know, have not endenizened themselves (nor possibly ever will) in the national heart, so as to become stock books—it is good to possess these in durable and costly covers. I do not care for a First Folio of Shakspeare. I rather prefer the common editions of Howe and Tonson, without notes, and with plates, which, being so execrably bad, serve as maps, or modest remembrancers, to the text; and without pretending to any supposable emulation with it, are so much better than the Shakspeare gallery engravings, which did. I have a community of feeling with my countrymen about his Plays, and I like those editions of him best, which have been oftenest tumbled about and handled. On the contrary, I cannot read Beaumont and Fletcher but in Folio. The Octavo editions are painful to look at. I have no sympathy with them. If they were as much read as the current editions of the other poet, I should prefer them in that shape to the older one. I do not know a more heartless sight than the reprint of the *Anatomy of Melancholy*. What need was there of unearthing the bones of that fantastic old great man, to expose them in a winding-sheet of the newest fashion to modern censure? what hapless stationer could dream of Burton ever becoming popular?—The wretched Malone could not do worse, when he bribed the sexton of Stratford church to let him white-wash the painted effigy of old Shakspeare, which stood there, in rude but lively fashion depicted, to the very colour of the cheek, the eye, the eye-brow, hair, the very dress he used to wear—the only authentic testimony we had, however imperfect, of these curious parts and parcels of him. They covered him over with a coat of white paint. By—, if I had been a justice of peace for Warwickshire, I would have clapt both commentator and sexton fast in the stocks, for a pair of meddling sacrilegious varlets.

I think I see them at their work—these sapient trouble-tombs.

Shall I be thought fantastical, if I confess, that the names of some of our poets sound sweeter, and have a finer relish to the ear—to mine, at least—than that of Milton or of Shakspeare? It may be, that the latter are more staled and rung upon in common discourse. The sweetest names, and which carry a perfume in the mention, are, Kit Marlowe, Drayton, Drummond of Hawthornden, and Cowley.

Much depends upon when and where you read a book. In the five or six impatient minutes, before the dinner is quite ready, who would think of taking up the *Fairy Queen* for a stop-gap, or volume of Bishop Andrewes' sermons?

Milton almost requires a solemn service of music to be played before you enter upon him. But he brings his music, to which, who listens, had need bring docile thoughts, and purged ears.

Winter evenings—the world shut out—with less of ceremony the gentle Shakspeare enters. At such a season, *The Tempest*, or his own *Winter's Tale*—

These two poets you cannot avoid reading aloud—to yourself, or (as it chances) to some single person listening. More than one—and it degenerates into an audience.

Books of quick interest, that hurry on for incidents, are for the eye to glide over only. It will not do to read them out. I could never listen to even the better kind of modern novels without extreme irksomeness.

A newspaper, read out, is intolerable. In some of the Bank offices it is the custom (to save so much individual time) for one of the clerks—who is the best scholar—to commence upon the *Times*, or the *Chronicle*, and recite its entire contents aloud *pro bono publico*. With every advantage of lungs and elocution, the effect is singularly vapid. In barbers' shops and public-houses a fellow will get up, and spell out a paragraph, which he communicates as some discovery. Another follows with his selection. So the entire journal transpires at length by piece-meal. Seldom-readers are slow readers, and, without this expedient no one in the company would probably ever travel through the contents of a whole paper.

Newspapers always excite curiosity. No one ever lays one down without a feeling of disappointment.

What an eternal time that gentleman in black, at Nando's, keeps the paper! I am sick of hearing the waiter bawling out incessantly, "the *Chronicle* is in hand, Sir."

Coming in to an inn at night—having ordered your supper—what can be more delightful than to find lying in

the window-seat, left there time out of mind by the care-
lessness of some former guest—two or three numbers
of the old *Town and Country Magazine*, with its amusing
tête-à-tête pictures—"The Royal Lover and Lady G—;"
"The Melting Platonic and the old Beau,"—and such like
antiquated scandal? Would you exchange it—at that time,
and in that place—for a better book?

Poor Tobin, who latterly fell blind, did not regret it
so much for the weightier kinds of reading—the *Paradise Lost*, or *Comus*, he could have read to him—but he
missed the pleasure of skimming over with his own eye
a magazine, or a light pamphlet.

I should not care to be caught in the serious avenues
of some cathedral alone, and reading *Candide*.

I do not remember a more whimsical surprise than
having been once detected—by a familiar damsel—
reclined at my ease upon the grass, on Primrose Hill
(her Cythera), reading—*Pamela*. There was nothing in
the book to make a man seriously ashamed at the expo-
sure; but as she seated herself down by me, and seemed
determined to read in company, I could have wished it
had been—any other book. We read on very sociably for
a few pages; and, not finding the author much to her
taste, she got up, and—went away. Gentle casuist, I leave
it to thee to conjecture, whether the blush (for there

46

was one between us) was the property of the nymph or the swain in this dilemma. From me you shall never get the secret.

I am not much a friend to out-of-doors reading. I cannot settle my spirits to it. I knew a Unitarian minister, who was generally to be seen upon Snow-hill (as yet Skinner's-street was not), between the hours of ten and eleven in the morning, studying a volume of Lardner. I own this to have been a strain of abstraction beyond my reach. I used to admire how he sidled along, keeping clear of secular contacts. An illiterate encounter with a porter's knot, or a bread basket, would have quickly put to flight all the theology I am master of, and have left me worse than indifferent to the five points.

There is a class of street-readers, whom I can never contemplate without affection—the poor gentry, who, not having wherewithal to buy or hire a book, filch a little learning at the open stalls—the owner, with his hard eye, casting envious looks at them all the while, and thinking when they will have done. Venturing tenderly, page after page, expecting every moment when he shall interpose his interdict, and yet unable to deny themselves the gratification, they "snatch a fearful joy." Martin B—, in this way, by daily fragments, got through two volumes of *Clarissa*, when the stall-keeper damped his laudable ambition, by asking him (it was in his younger days) whether he meant to purchase the work. M. declares, that under no circumstances of his life did he ever peruse a book with half the satisfaction which he took in those uneasy snatches. A quaint poetess of our day has moralized upon this subject in two very touching but homely stanzas.

The Two Boys

I saw a boy with eager eye
Open a book upon a stall
And read, as he'd devour it all;
Which when the stall-man did espy,

Soon to the boy I heard him call,
"You, Sir, you never buy a book,
Therefore in one you shall not look."
The boy pass'd slowly on, and with a sigh
He wish'd he never had been taught to read,
Then of the old churl's books he should have had
    no need.

Of sufferings the poor have many,
Which never can the rich annoy:
I soon perceiv'd another boy,
Who look'd as if he'd not had any

Food, for that day at least—enjoy
The sight of cold meat in a tavern larder.
This boy's case, then thought I, is surely harder,
Thus hungry, longing, thus without a penny
Beholding choice of dainty-dressed meat:
No wonder if he wish he ne'er had learn'd to eat.

*Tolstoy is an interesting and stimulating writer,
but an exceedingly unsafe moral adviser ❡*

Books for Holidays in the Open

Theodore Roosevelt

*Explorer, writer, naturalist and 26th President of the United
States, Theodore Roosevelt (1858–1919) is also arguably the
country's best-read President. A poster boy for the speed reading movement, he whizzed through a book a day, often written
in various different languages. Although Roosevelt disliked
the idea of "must read" book lists, believing one size did not
fit all—"The room for choice is so limitless it seems absurd to
try to make catalogues which shall be supposed to appeal to
all the best thinkers"—he was a keen supporter of short stories
and poetry.*

*A childhood asthmatic, Roosevelt became a great believer
in the benefits of the great outdoors and the importance of
physical exercise—he once described himself to be "as strong
as a bull moose" and the moniker stuck, both to him and the*

short-lived political Progressive Party he formed. As well as a prolific letter writer, Roosevelt also wrote books on naval history, Oliver Cromwell, and the "Summer Birds of the Adirondacks". The piece below comes from his book A Book Lover's Holidays in the Open *(1916). Other robust chapters include "A cougar hunt on the rim of the Grand Canyon" and "Primitive Man and the horse, the lion and the elephant".*

I am sometimes asked what books I advise men or women to take on holidays in the open. With the reservation of long trips, where bulk is of prime consequence, I can only answer: The same books one would read at home. Such an answer generally invites the further question as to what books I read when at home. To this question I am afraid my answer cannot be so instructive as it ought to be, for I have never followed any plan in reading which would apply to all persons under all circumstances; and indeed it seems to me that no plan can be laid down that will be generally applicable. If a man is not fond of books, to him reading of any kind will be drudgery. I most sincerely commiserate such a person, but I do not know how to help him. If a man or a woman is fond of books he or she will naturally seek the books that the mind and soul demand. Suggestions of a possibly helpful character can be made by outsiders, but only suggestions; and they will probably be helpful about in proportion to the outsider's knowledge of the mind and soul of the person to be helped.

Of course, if any one finds that he never reads serious literature, if all his reading is frothy and trashy, he would do well to try to train himself to like books that the general agreement of cultivated and sound-thinking persons has placed among the classics. It is as discreditable to the mind to be unfit for sustained mental effort as it is to the body of a young man to be unfit for sustained physical effort. Let man or woman, young man or girl, read some good author, say Gibbon or Macaulay, until sustained mental effort brings power to enjoy the books worth enjoying. When this has been achieved the man can soon trust himself to pick out for himself the particular good books which appeal to him.

The equation of personal taste is as powerful in reading as in eating; and within certain broad limits the matter is merely one of individual preference, having nothing to do with the quality either of the book or of the reader's mind. I like apples, pears, oranges, pineapples, and peaches. I dislike bananas, alligator-pears, and prunes. The first fact is certainly not to my credit, although it is to my advantage; and the second at least does not show moral turpitude. At times in the tropics I have been exceedingly sorry I could not learn to like bananas, and on round-ups, in the cow country in the old days, it was even more unfortunate not to like prunes; but I simply could not make myself like either, and that was all there was to it.

In the same way I read over and over again *Guy Mannering*, *The Antiquary*, *Pendennis*, *Vanity Fair*, *Our Mutual Friend*, and *The Pickwick Papers*; whereas I make heavy weather of most parts of *The Fortunes of Nigel*, *Esmond*, and *The Old Curiosity Shop*—to mention only books I have tried to read during the last month. I have no question that the latter three books are as good as the first six; doubtless for some people they are better; but I do not like them, any more than I like prunes or bananas.

In the same way I read and reread *Macbeth* and *Othello*; but not *King Lear* nor *Hamlet*. I know perfectly well that the latter are as wonderful as the former—I wouldn't venture to admit my shortcomings regarding them if I couldn't proudly express my appreciation of the other two! But at my age I might as well own up, at least to myself, to my limitations, and read the books I thoroughly enjoy.

But this does not mean permitting oneself to like what is vicious or even simply worthless. If any man finds that he cares to read *Bel Ami*, he will do well to keep a watch on the reflex centres of his moral nature, and to brace himself with a course of Eugene Brieux or Henry Bordeaux. If he does not care for *Anna Karenina*, *War and Peace*, *Sebastopol*, and *The Cossacks* he misses much; but if he cares for the *Kreutzer Sonata* he had better make up his mind that for pathological reasons he will be wise thereafter to avoid Tolstoy entirely. Tolstoy is an interesting and stimulating writer, but an exceedingly unsafe moral adviser.

It is clear that the reading of vicious books for pleasure should be eliminated. It is no less clear that trivial and vulgar books do more damage than can possibly be offset by any entertainment they yield. There remain enormous masses of books, of which no one man can read more than a limited number, and among which each reader should choose those which meet his own particular needs. There is no such thing as a list of "the hundred best books," or the "best five-foot library."

Dozens of series of excellent books, one hundred to each series, can be named, all of reasonably equal merit and each better for many readers than any of the others; and probably not more than half a dozen books would appear in all these lists. As for a "five-foot library," scores can readily be devised, each of which at some given time, for some given man, under certain conditions, will be best. But to attempt to create such a library that shall be of universal value is foreordained to futility.

Within broad limits, therefore, the reader's personal and individual taste must be the guiding factor. I like hunting books and books of exploration and adventure. I do not ask any one else to like them. I distinctly do not hold my own preferences as anything whatever but individual preferences; and this chapter is to be accepted as confessional rather than didactic. With this understanding I admit a liking for novels where something happens; and even among these novels I can neither explain nor justify why I like some and do not like others; why, among the novels of Sienkiewicz, I cannot stand *Quo Vadis*, and never tire of *With Fire and Sword*, *Pan Michael*, *The Deluge* and *The Knights of the Cross*.

Of course, I know that the best critics scorn the demand among novel readers for "the happy ending." Now, in really great books—in an epic like Milton's, in dramas like those of Æschylus and Sophocles—I am entirely willing to accept and even demand tragedy, and also in some poetry that cannot be called great, but not in good, readable novels, of sufficient length to enable me to get interested in the hero and heroine!

There is enough of horror and grimness and sordid squalor in real life with which an active man has to grapple; and when I turn to the world of literature—of books considered as books, and not as instruments of my profession—I do not care to study suffering unless for some sufficient purpose. It is only a very exceptional novel which I will read if He does not marry Her; and even in exceptional novels I much prefer this consummation. I am not defending my attitude. I am merely stating it.

Therefore it would be quite useless for me to try to explain why I read certain books. As to how and when, my answers must be only less vague. I almost always read a good deal in the evening; and if the rest of the evening is occupied I can at least get half an hour before going to bed. But all kinds of odd moments turn up during even a busy day, in which it is possible to enjoy a book; and then there are rainy afternoons in the country in autumn, and stormy days in winter, when one's work outdoors is finished and after wet clothes have been changed for dry, the rocking-chair in front of the open wood-fire simply demands an accompanying book.

Railway and steamboat journeys were, of course, predestined through the ages as aids to the enjoyment of reading. I have always taken books with me when on hunting and exploring trips. In such cases the literature should be reasonably heavy, in order that it may last. You can under these conditions read Herbert Spencer, for example, or the writings of Turgot, or a German study of the Mongols, or even a German edition of Aristophanes, with erudite explanations of the jokes, as you never would if surrounded by less formidable authors in your own library; and when you do reach the journey's end you grasp with eager appetite at old magazines, or at the lightest of literature.

Then, if one is worried by all kinds of men and events— during critical periods in administrative office, or at national conventions, or during congressional investigations, or in hard-fought political campaigns—it is the greatest relief and unalloyed delight to take up some really good, some really enthralling book—Tacitus, Thucydides, Herodotus, Polybius, or Goethe, Keats, Gray, or Lowell—and lose all memory of everything grimy, and of the baseness that must be parried or conquered.

Like everyone else, I am apt to read in streaks. If I get interested in any subject I read different books connected with it, and probably also read books on subjects suggested by it. Having read Carlyle's *Frederick the Great*—with its splendid description of the battles, and of the unyielding courage and thrifty resourcefulness of the iron-tempered King; and with its screaming deification of able brutality in the name of morality, and its practise of the suppression and falsification of the truth under the pretence of preaching veracity—I turned to Macaulay's essay on this subject, and found that the historian whom it has been the fashion of the intellectuals to patronize or deride showed a much sounder philosophy, and an infinitely greater appreciation of and devotion to truth than was shown by the loquacious apostle of the doctrine of reticence.

Then I took up Waddington's *Guerre de Sept Ans*; then I read all I could about Gustavus Adolphus; and, gradually dropping everything but the military side, I got hold of quaint little old histories of Eugene of Savoy and Turenne. In similar fashion my study of and delight in Mahan sent me further afield, to read queer old volumes about De Ruyter and the daring warrior-merchants of the Hansa, and to study, as well as I could, the feats of Suffren and Tegethoff. I did not need to study Farragut.

Mahaffy's books started me to reread—in translation, alas!—the post-Athenian Greek authors. After Ferrero I did the same thing as regards the Latin authors, and then industriously read all kinds of modern writers on the same period, finishing with Oman's capital essay on *Seven Roman Statesmen*. Gilbert Murray brought me back from Greek history to Greek literature, and thence by a natural suggestion to parts of the Old Testament, to the *Nibelungenlied*, to The Roland lay and the chansons de gestes, to *Beowulf*, and finally to the great Japanese hero-tale, the story of the *Forty-Nine Ronins*.

I read Burroughs too often to have him suggest anything save himself; but I am exceedingly glad that Charles Sheldon has arisen to show what a hunter-naturalist, who adds the ability of the writer to the ability of the trained observer and outdoor adventurer, can do for our last great wilderness, Alaska. From Sheldon I turned to Stewart Edward White, and then began to wander afar, with

Herbert Ward's *Voice from the Congo*, and Mary Kingsley's writings, and Hudson's *El Ombu*, and Cunningham Grahame's sketches of South America. A re-reading of *The Federalist* led me to Burke, to Trevelyan's history of Fox and of our own Revolution, to Lecky; and finally by way of Malthus and Adam Smith and Lord Acton and Bagehot to my own contemporaries, to Ross and George Alger.

Even in pure literature, having nothing to do with history, philosophy, sociology, or economy, one book will often suggest another, so that one finds one has unconsciously followed a regular course of reading. Once I travelled steadily from Montaigne through Addison, Swift, Steele, Lamb, Irving, and Lowell to Crothers and Kenneth Grahame—and if it be objected that some of these *could* not have suggested the others I can only answer that they *did* suggest them.

I suppose that everyone passes through periods during which he reads no poetry; and some people, of whom I am one, also pass through periods during which they voraciously devour poets of widely different kinds. Now it will be Horace and Pope; now Schiller, Scott, Longfellow, Körner; now Bret Harte or Kipling; now Shelley or Herrick or Tennyson; now Poe and Coleridge; and again, Emerson or Browning or Whitman. Sometimes one wishes to read for the sake of contrast. To me Owen Wister is the writer I wish when I am hungry with the memories of lonely mountains, of vast sunny plains with seas of wind-rippled grass, of springing wild creatures, and lithe, sun-tanned men who ride with utter ease on ungroomed, half-broken horses. But when I lived much in cow camps I often carried a volume of Swinburne, as a kind of antiseptic to alkali dust, tepid, muddy water, frying-pan bread, sow-belly bacon, and the too-infrequent washing of sweat-drenched clothing.

Fathers and mothers who are wise can train their children first to practise, and soon to like, the sustained mental application necessary to enjoy good books. They will do well also to give each boy or girl the mastery of at least some one foreign language, so that at least one other great literature, in addition to our own noble English literature, shall be open to him or her. Modern languages are taught so easily and readily that whoever really desires to learn one of them can soon achieve sufficient command of it to read ordinary books with reasonable ease; and then it is a mere matter of practise for anyone to become able thoroughly to enjoy the beauty and wisdom which knowledge of the new tongue brings.

Now and then one's soul thirsts for laughter. I cannot imagine any one's taking a course in humorous writers, but just as little can I sympathize with the man who does not enjoy them at times—from Sydney Smith to John Phœnix and Artemus Ward, and from these to Stephen Leacock. Mark Twain at his best stands a little apart, almost as much so as Joel Chandler Harris. Oliver Wendell Holmes, of course, is the laughing philosopher, the humorist at his very highest, even if we use the word "humour" only in its most modern and narrow sense.

A man with a real fondness for books of various kinds will find that his varying moods determine which of these books he at the moment needs. On the afternoon when Stevenson represents the luxury of enjoyment it may safely be assumed that Gibbon will not. The mood that is met by Napier's *Peninsular War*, or Marbot's memoirs, will certainly not be met by Hawthorne or Jane Austen. Parkman's *Montcalm and Wolfe*, Motley's histories of the Dutch Republic, will hardly fill the soul on a day when one turns naturally to the *Heimskringla*; and there is a sense of disconnection if after the *Heimskringla* one takes up *The Oxford Book of French Verse*.

Another matter which within certain rather wide limits each reader must settle for himself is the dividing line between (1) not knowing anything about current books, and (2) swamping one's soul in the sea of vapidity which overwhelms him who reads *only* "the last new books." To me the heading employed by some reviewers when they speak of "books of the week" comprehensively damns both the books themselves and the reviewer who is willing to notice them. I would much rather see the heading "books of the year before last." A book of the year before last which is still worth noticing would probably be worth reading; but one only entitled to be called a book of the week had better be tossed into the wastebasket at once. Still, there are plenty of new books which are not of permanent value but which nevertheless are worth more or less careful reading; partly because it is well to know something of what especially interests the mass of our fellows, and partly because these books, although of ephemeral worth, may really set forth something genuine in a fashion which for the moment stirs the hearts of all of us.

Books of more permanent value may, because of the very fact that they possess literary interest, also yield consolation of a non-literary kind. If any executive grows exasperated over the shortcomings of the legislative body with which he deals, let him study Macaulay's account of the way William was treated by his parliaments as soon as the latter found that, thanks to his efforts, they were no longer in immediate danger from foreign foes; it is illuminating. If any man feels too gloomy about the degeneracy of our people from the standards of their forefathers, let him read *Martin Chuzzlewit*; it will be consoling.

If the attitude of this nation toward foreign affairs and military preparedness at the present day seems disheartening, a study of the first fifteen years of the nineteenth century will at any rate give us whatever comfort we can extract from the fact that our great-grandfathers were no less foolish than we are.

Nor need any one confine himself solely to the affairs of the United States. If he becomes tempted to idealize the past, if sentimentalists seek to persuade him that the "ages of faith," the twelfth and thirteenth centuries, for instance, were better than our own, let him read any trustworthy book on the subject—Lea's *History of the Inquisition*, for instance, or Coulton's abridgment of Salimbene's memoirs. He will be undeceived and will be devoutly thankful that his lot has been cast in the present age, in spite of all its faults.

It would be hopeless to try to enumerate all the books I read, or even all the kinds. The foregoing is a very imperfect answer to a question which admits of only such an answer.

How pure the joy, when first my hands unfold
The small, rare volume, black with tarnish'd gold! ❡

Bibliomania

John Ferriar

Dr John Ferriar (1761–1815) was not only a steadfast cam-
paigner for the improvement of public healthcare for the poor
in the late 18th and early 19th centuries, he is also acclaimed
as the inventor of the term "bibliomania" which he coined
at the time of a Europe-wide boom in book collecting among
aristocrats and the middle-classes. Born in Oxnam in the
Scottish borders, he became a leading physician at the Man-
chester Infirmary. Ferriar concentrated initially on typhoid but
increasingly on mental problems and developed an early psy-
chiatric-based approach to illness. In this light-hearted poem
(1809) to his friend and compulsive book collector Richard
Heber—a member of the world's oldest society of bibliophiles,
The Roxburghe Club, which continues to meet today—he took
humorous aim at rich book collectors who took their obsession

too far. Heber was in fact one of the founders of the Roxburghe (for an excellent overview see The Early Roxburghe Club 1812–1835: Book Club Pioneers and the Advancement of English Literature *by Shayne Husbands) and his library was described by fellow member Sir Walter Scott as the finest in the world. When he died, it held about 150,000 books plus numerous pamphlets at his homes in England and around Europe. Ferriar's poem inspired the Reverend Thomas Dibdin, who founded the exclusive Roxburghe gatherings, to write the seminal early work on the subject a year later,* Bibliomania or Book Madness.

THE
BIBLIOMANIA,
AN
EPISTLE,
TO RICHARD HEBER, ESQ.
BY
JOHN FERRIAR, M. D.

Hic, inquis, Veto quisquam faxit Oletum.
Pinge duos Angues:—[1]

Pers. Sat. 1. *l.* 108.

WHAT wild desires, what restless torments seize
The hapless man, who feels the book-disease,
If niggard Fortune cramp his gen'rous mind,
And Prudence quench the Spark by heaven assign'd!
With wistful glance his aching eyes behold
The Princeps-copy, clad in blue and gold,
Where the tall Book-case, with partition thin,

---

1 "Here, you say, I forbid anyone to relieve themselves. Paint two
snakes:—" The practise of painting two snakes, a sacred symbol, on
buildings was to dissuade the public from "relieving themselves"
on its walls—in much the same way as the adornment of crosses
on a wall might convince a reveller to find another, less seemingly
sacred, spot for their "relief".

Displays, yet guards the tempting charms within:
So great Facardin view'd, as sages tell,
Fair Crystalline immur'd in lucid cell.

Not thus the few, by happier fortune grac'd,
And blest, like you, with talents, wealth and taste,
Who gather nobly, with judicious hand,
The Muse's treasures from each letter'd strand.
For you the Monk illumin'd his pictur'd page,
For you the press defies the Spoils of age;
FAUSTUS for you infernal tortures bore,
For you ERASMUS starv'd on Adria's shore.
The FOLIO-ALDUS loads your happy Shelves,
And dapper ELZEVIRS, like fairy elves,
Shew their light forms amidst the well-gilt Twelves:
In slender type the GIOLITOS shine,
And bold BODONI stamps his Roman line.
For you the LOUVRE opes its regal doors,
And either DIDOT lends his brilliant stores:
With faultless types, and costly sculptures bright,
IBARRA's Quixote charms your ravish'd sight:
LABORDE in splendid tablets shall explain
Thy beauties, glorious, tho' unhappy SPAIN!
O, hallowed name, the theme of future years,
Embalm'd in Patriot-blood, and England's tears,

Be thine fresh honours from the tuneful tongue,
By Isis' streams which mourning Zion sung!

But devious oft' from ev'ry classic Muse,
The keen Collector meaner paths will choose:
And first the Margin's breadth his soul employs,
Pure, snowy, broad, the type of nobler joys.
In vain might HOMER roll the tide of song,
Or HORACE smile, or TULLY charm the throng;
If crost by Pallas' ire, the trenchant blade
Or too oblique, or near, the edge invade,
The Bibliomane exclaims, with haggard eye,
"No Margin!" turns in haste, and scorns to buy.
He turns where PYBUS rears his Atlas-head,
Or MADOC's mass conceals its veins of lead.
The glossy lines in polish'd order stand,
While the vast margin spreads on either hand,
Like Russian wastes, that edge the frozen deep,
Chill with pale glare, and lull to mortal sleep.

Or English books, neglected and forgot,
Excite his wish in many a dusty lot:
Whatever trash Midwinter gave to day,
Or Harper's rhyming sons, in paper gray,
At ev'ry auction, bent on fresh supplies,

He cons his Catalogue with anxious eyes:
Where'er the slim Italics mark the page,
Curious and rare his ardent mind engage.
Unlike the Swans, in Tuscan Song display'd,
He hovers eager o'er Oblivion's Shade,
To snatch obscurest names from endless night,
To give COKAIN or FLETCHER back to light.
In red Morocco drest he loves to boast
The bloody murder, or the yelling ghost;
Or dismal ballads, sung to crowds of old,
Now cheaply bought for thrice their weight in gold.
Yet to th'unhonoured dead be Satire just;
Some flow'rs "smell sweet, and blossom in their dust."
'Tis thus ev'n SHIRLEY boasts a golden line,
And LOVELACE strikes, by fits, a note divine.
Th'unequal gleams like midnight-lightnings play,
And deepen'd gloom succeeds, in place of day.
But human bliss still meets some envious storm;
He droops to view his PAYNTER's mangled form:
Presumptuous grief, while pensive Taste repines
O'er the frail relics of her Attic Shrines!
O for that power, for which magicians vye,
To look through earth, and secret hoards descry!
I'd spurn such gems as Marinel beheld,
And all the wealth Aladdin's cavern held,

Might I divine in what mysterious gloom
The rolls of sacred bards have found their tomb:
Beneath what mould'ring tower, or waste champain,
Is his MENANDER, sweetest of the train;
Where rests ANTIMACHUS' forgotten lyre,
Where gently SAPPHO's still seductive fire;
Or he, whom chief the laughing Muses own,
Yet skill'd with softest accents to bemoan
Sweet Philomel, in strains so like her own.
The menial train has prov'd the Scourge of wit,
Ev'n OMAR burnt less Science than the spit.
Earthquakes and wars remit their deadly rage,
But ev'ry feast demands some fated page.
Ye towers of Julius, ye alone remain
Of all the piles that saw our nation's stain.
When HARRY's sway opprest the groaning realm,
And Lust and Rapine seiz'd the wav'ring helm.
Then ruffian-hands defaced the sacred fanes,
Their saintly statues, and their storied panes;
Then from the chest, with ancient art embost,
The Penman's pious scrolls were rudely tost;
Then richest manuscripts, profusely spread,
The brawnt Churl's devouring Oven fed:
And thence Collectors date the heav'nly ire,
That wrapt Augusta's domes in sheets of fire.

Taste, tho' misled, may yet some purpose gain,
But fashion guides a book-compelling train.
Once, far apart from Learning's moping crew,
The travell'd beau display'd his red-heel'd shoe,
Till ORFORD rose, and told of rhiming Peers,
Repeating noble words to polish'd ears;
Taught the gay croud to prize a flutt'ring name,
In trifling toil'd, nor "blush'd to find it fame."
The letter'd fop now takes a larger scope,
With classic furniture, design'd by HOPE,
(HOPE, whom Upholst'rers eye with mute despair,
The doughty pedant of an elbow-chair;)
Now warm'd by ORFORD and by GRANGER school'd,
In Paper-books, superbly gilt and tool'd,
He pastes, from injur'd volumes snipt away,
His English Heads, in chronicled array.
Torn from their destin'd page, (unworthy meed
Of knightly counsel, and heroic deed)
Not FAITHORNE's stroke, nor FIELD's own types
   can save
The gallant VERES, and one-eyed OGLE brave.
Indignant readers seek the image fled,
And curse the busy fool, who wants a head.

Proudly he shews, with many a smile elate,
The scrambling subjects of the private plate;
While Time their actions and their names bereaves,
They grin forever in the guarded leaves.

Like Poets, born, in vain Collectors strive
To cross their Fate, and learn the art to thrive.
Like Cacus, bent to tame their struggling will,
The tyrant-passion drags them backward still:
Ev'n I, debarr'd of ease, and studious hours,
Confess, mid' anxious toil, its lurking pow'rs.
How pure the joy, when first my hands unfold
The small, rare volume, black with tarnish'd gold!
The Eye skims restless, like the roving bee,
O'er flowers of wit, or song, or repartee,
While sweet as Springs, new-bubbling from the stone,
Glides through the breast some pleasing theme
    unknown.
Now dipt in ROSSI's terse and classic style,
His harmless tales awake a transient smile.
Now BOUCHET's motley stores my thoughts arrest,
With wond'rous reading, and with learned jest.
Bouchet, whose tomes a grateful line demand,
The valued gift of STANLEY's lib'ral hand.

Now sadly pleased, through faded Rome I stray,
And mix regrets with gently DU BELLAY;
Or turn, with keen delight, the curious page,
Where hardy Pasquin braves the Pontiff's rage.

But D−−−−−n's strains should tell the sad reverse,
When Business calls, invet'rate foe to verse!
Tell how "the Demon claps his iron hands,"
"Waves his lank locks, and scours along the lands."
Though wintry blasts, or summer's fire I go,
To scenes of danger, and to sights of woe.
Ev'n when to Margate ev'ry Cockney roves,
And brainsick poets long for shelt'ring groves,
Whose lofty shades exclude the noontide glow,
While Zephyrs breathe, and waters trill below,
Me rigid Fate averts, by tasks like these,
From heav'nly musings, and from letter'd ease.

Such wholesome checks the better Genius sends,
From dire rehearsals to protect our friends:
Else when the social rites our joys renew,
The stuff'd Portfolio would alarm your view,
Whence volleying rhimes your patience would
    o'ercome,
And, spite of kindness, drive you early home.

So when the traveller's hasty footsteps glide
Near smoking lava, on Vesuvio's side,
Hoarse-mutt'ring thunders from the depths proceed,
And spouting fires incite his eager speed.
Appall'd he flies, while rattling show'rs invade,
Invoking ev'ry Saint for instant aid:
Breathless, amaz'd, he seeks the distant shore,
And vows to tempt the dang'rous gulph no more.

Books used intemperately to excess become most dangerous drugs ❡

The Uses of Reading

Rudyard Kipling

Best known for his poetry and novels such as Kim *and* The Jungle Book, *Rudyard Kipling (1865–1936) also frequently made speeches for a wide variety of audiences and on the numerous topics in which he was interested, including politics and empire, culture, and medicine. Not hugely enthusiastic about public speaking, he nevertheless had a conversational and light style without oratorical bangs and whizzes (on YouTube you can see and listen to a snippet of him giving a talk at bit.ly/kiplingspeech), often learning his speeches before giving them. He collected 31 of his speeches made between 1906 and 1927 and published them as* A Book of Words *(1928). These cover his key interests such as "Imperial Relations", "The Spirit of the Navy", and "Our Indian Troops in France", as well as the one reproduced below given to pupils at Wellington College in May 1912 which was originally called "The Possible Advantages of Reading". He spoke to an audience of around 50 boys including his teenage son John and, according to the school magazine, it made quite an impression on the listeners. More of his speeches are available at www.kiplingsociety.co.uk and in a second collection called* A Second Book of Words *(2008).*

You have done me the honour of asking me to read a paper to your society this evening. Before I begin, I may as well confess that this is the first time I have ever read a paper in school since I was a member of the Natural History Society at my old school, when, for reasons which I need not explain to you, I had to read a paper whether I liked it or not.

It is one thing to write and quite another thing to read. And that brings me directly to what I wanted to speak about—which is the use and value of a little reading.

There is, or there was, an idea that reading in itself is a virtuous and holy deed. I can't quite agree with this, because it seems to me that the mere fact of a man's being fond of reading proves nothing one way or the other. He may be constitutionally lazy; or he may be overstrained, and so take refuge in a book to rest himself. He may be full of curiosity and wonder about the life on which he is just entering; and for that reason may plunge into any and every book he can lay hands on, in order to get information about things that are puzzling him, or frightening him, or interesting him.

Now, I am a very long way from saying that literature ought to be a chief or a leading interest in most men's lives, or even in the life of a nation. But a man who goes into life with no knowledge of the literature of his own country and without a certain acquaintance with the classics and the value of words, is as heavily handicapped as a man who takes up sports or games without knowing what has been done in these particular sports or games, before he came on the scene. He doesn't know the records and so he can't have any standards. I have a book at home that gives a summary with diagrams, of practically every attempt at perpetual-motion machines that have ever been invented for the last two hundred years. It was compiled for the purpose of saving inventors trouble; and the compiler says in his preface: "One of the grossest fallacies of the mind is that of taking for granted that ideas of mechanical construction, apparently the result of accident, must of necessity be quite original. The most doubtful originality is that which the inventor attributes to his ignorance of all previous plans coupled with his isolated position in life."

There you have precisely the position of the man who has no knowledge of literature—ignorant that is, of all previous plans. Such a man is more likely than not to waste his own time and the patience of his friends—perhaps even to endanger the safety of the community—by inventing schemes for the conduct of his own, or his neighbours' affairs, which have been tried, found wanting, and laid aside any time these thousand years; and the record of which—the diagram and specification, so to say, of which—he could turn to if he had only taken the trouble to read.

One of the hardest things to realise, specially for a young man, is that our forefathers were living men who really knew something, I would go further and say they knew a very great deal. Indeed, I should not be surprised if they knew quite as much as we do about the things that really concern men. What each generation forgets is that while the words which it uses to describe ideas are always changing, the ideas themselves do not change so quickly, nor are those ideas in any sense new.

If we pay no attention to words whatever, we may become like the isolated gentleman who invents a new perpetual-motion machine on old lines in ignorance of all previous plans, and then is surprised that it doesn't work. If we confine our attention entirely to the slang of the day—that is to say, if we devote ourselves exclusively to modern literature—we get to think the world is progressing when it is only repeating itself. In both cases we are likely to be deceived, and what is more important, to deceive others. Therefore, it is advisable for us in our own interests, quite apart from considerations of personal amusement, to concern ourselves occasionally with a certain amount of our national literature drawn from all ages. I say from all ages, because it is only when one reads what men wrote long ago that one realizes how absolutely modern the best of the old things are.

About fifteen hundred years ago some early Anglo-Saxon writer saw, or heard about (I imagine in those days men had generally seen what they wrote about) the ruins of an old Roman city half buried and going to pieces in the jungle somewhere in the south of England; with its walls split and falling; its roofs stripped of its tiles; its towers fallen, and all its luxurious baths and heating arrangements open to the air. The man begins to wonder about the people who built all this magnificence and he says:

> Earth's grasp holdeth
> The mighty workmen
> Worn away; lorn away [geworen forloren]
> In the grip of the grave.

Then he thinks of the strong man who commanded the place when it was first built—most likely it was a Roman prefect—and he describes him:

> Gorgeous and gold-bright,
> Gaudily jewelled,

> Haughty and wine-hot,
> Shining in armour.

And as the poem goes on, we can almost see the band of Anglo-Saxon hunters or raiders, who have scrambled through the bushes, and stand, picking the thorns out of their legs, in the presence of this great, mysterious dead city. There is one touch which is exactly what hot and dirty men would think, when they saw all the paraphernalia of the old Roman baths:

> There stood courts of stone.
> The steam hotly rushed,
> With a wide eddy,
> Between shut walls.
> There were the baths
> Hot to bathe in.
> That was a boon indeed!

The whole thing is as modern as to-day's evening paper—but with a freshness and a directness and a simplicity that isn't common in modern work.

I'll take another instance. About five hundred years ago, Chaucer wrote a poem on how a man ought to manage his life. The last verse of it—it is only three verses long—runs:

That thee is sent receive in buxomnesse [be thankful
    for what you get]
The wrestling of this world asketh a fall.
Here is no home—here is but wildernesse:
Forth pilgrime—forth beast from out thy stall!
Look up on high and thanke the God of all.
Weive thy lusts and let thy ghost thee lead [That
    means, keep yourself in hand and trust your spirit]
And truth shall thee deliver, it is no drede.

The whole thing absolutely covers the few facts in life that really matter.

A last instance. In the course of his wonderful career, Sir Walter Raleigh had occasion to write his opinion, as you may have to someday, on the value of forts for coast and harbour defence. Well, his practical experience showed him, what we forgot and only realized a few years ago, that mere forts on the land aren't enough to maintain an effective defence or blockade, unless they are supported by ships. And he says so. But he doesn't say it as you and I would. For some inscrutable reason

Elizabethans, apparently, could not put pen to paper without producing uncommonly good prose. So he gives his reasons and his experiences thus:

"In this age a valiant and judicious man-of-war will not fear to pass by the best appointed fort of Europe, with the help of a good tide and a leading gale of wind; no, though forty pieces of great artillery open their mouths against him, and threaten to tear him in pieces. It was not long since, that the Duke of Parma, besieging Antwerp and finding no possibility to master it otherwise than by famine, laid his cannon on the bank of the river so well to purpose that he thought it impossible for the least boat to pass. Yet the Hollanders and Zeelanders, not blown up by any wind of glory, but coming to find a good market for their butter and cheese—even the poor men attending their profit, when all things were extreme dear at Antwerp—passed in boats of ten or twelve tun, by the mouth of the duke's cannon in despight of them, when a strong westerly wind and flood favoured them. As also with a contrary wind and ebbing tide they returned back again. So he was forced in the end to build his stockade overthwart the river, to his marvellous trouble and charge. It is true, that where a fort is so set that there is no passing along beside it, or that ships are driven to turn upon a bow-line towards it, wanting all help of wind and tide; there, and in such places, it is of great use and fearful. Otherwise not."

Here I have given you three specimens of not exactly modern literature in three different keys; the first dealing with a concrete thing seen and brought home to a man's mind; the second describing a man's thoughts on the conduct of his own soul; and the third a practical man's plans for dealing with an actual situation—a piece, that is, of pure intellect.

But it is very possible that when you come to read them, these three specimens may not appeal to you. No matter. That is just a question of temperament; and a man is no more to be blamed for not caring for certain forms of literature than he is for not thriving on certain forms of food.

But your choice is practically illimitable; for the literature of our England is strewn from end to end with a prodigality that almost frightens one—strewn with gems and jewels and glories and beauties fitted to every conceivable need that can arise in the course of any human being's life. But we make very little use of them. That again is quite natural. If we could buy knowledge, prudence, forethought and all the elementary virtues out of sevenpenny editions of standard authors, we should long ago have become a race of unbearably perfect archangels. And we are still quite a little lower than the angels. None the less, it is possible that our reading, if so be we read wisely, may save us to a certain extent from some of the serious forms of trouble; or if we get into trouble, as we most certainly shall, may teach us how to come out of it decently.

Here is an instance, which has nothing to do directly with written words, that shows the extraordinary value of getting at another man's experience and using it. I was talking some time ago with our greatest General and he told me that when he went out first to India as a subaltern of Artillery, about seventeen years old, he was posted to his father's Command in Peshawur. A short time before that, his father had commanded a brigade in one of the big Frontier wars, which war, to put it gently, hadn't been a success. The general in charge of those operations had occupied a town and had put his guns in one place, his forage and his provisions in another, and had tried to hold more ground than he could with the troops at his disposal. Then the country rose round him and there was a series of regrettable incidents. (That was a campaign which, I have always thought, helped to bring on the Indian Mutiny.) Well, you can imagine how the young subaltern, sitting at the bottom of his father's table at Peshawur, must have heard the failure of the campaign discussed from every possible point of view by his father's comrades who had taken part in it—majors and colonels of the old hooka-smoking times of the early '50's. And you can think of 'em throwing him a word here and there in the middle of their talk and saying: "Look here, youngster, if you're ever caught in such and such a position, you do so-and-so".

Then, years later, this young subaltern of Artillery became a general commanding an army and, by the luck of war, he found himself on the identical ground and in the identical city under practically the same conditions that he had heard discussed in his youth, by the men who had taken part in the old war. He said, telling me the tale: "It all came back to me. I put my guns and my forage and my rations where I could lay my hands on 'em; and I took very good care not to try and hold more ground than I had troops for; and I settled in quite comfortably. I sent a wire to the Indian Government telling them exactly how long I could hold out for—and—that was all there was to it." Of course there was a lot more to it—there was his own genius—but you can see the tremendous advantage he had in having got his knowledge in his youth. True, it was hereditary knowledge—more sound, more adhesive than anything he was likely to have got out of a book.

But the main idea is in line with what I've been talking about.

If a man brings a good mind to what he reads he may become, as it were, the spiritual descendant to some extent of great men, and this link, this spiritual hereditary tie, may help to just kick the beam in the right direction at a vital crisis; or may keep him from drifting through the long slack times when, so to speak, we are only fielding and no balls are coming our way.

You know those curious half-waking dreams that one dreams, about one's future—a sort of story without words of the things we mean to do later on? They shade off into a vision of a gloriously successful career in our chosen line with all the world at our feet, recognizing at last what splendid fellows we were. Then we forgive all our enemies, after we've got our feet on their necks; take our seat either as a Viceroy or a legislator or a Field-Marshal or some insignificant trifle of that kind—and then we wake! Sometimes the dreams have a knack of coming true. A man does achieve something out of the ordinary; finds himself saddled with tremendous responsibilities and expected to play up to a new part. Well, that is the time that he should have provided himself with all the knowledge and strength that can be drawn from noble books, so that whatever has happened to him may not be overwhelming nor unexpected. And to do that, to keep his soul fit for all chances, a man should associate at certain times in his soul (there is no need to tell everyone about it) with the best, the most balanced, the largest, finest, and most honourable and capable minds of the past. It may be a snobbish way of putting it, but a man should know "the right people" in the great world of books, and they'll help to show him what the world really means. Men will tell you that the days are over when one can suddenly be called to power and glory. Don't you believe it! A chance may open suddenly in front of one at a minute's notice. A man's superior may die and leave him in temporary charge of a district half the size of France with ten million people in it. A flood, a storm, an outbreak of sickness may change a man's position and outlook and responsibility between breakfast and lunch. One never knows one's luck, but one ought always to be ready for it. I have seen men very little over twenty get one chance and take it. To give you an instance, I happened to be in Bloemfontein after a "regrettable incident" called Sanna's Post—where we lost five or six hundred men and several guns in a little ambush. I met one of the survivors a few hours after the thing had happened. He had done very well in a losing game, and he had come out of it, looking exactly like a man after the last half of a really hectic footer game. His clothes were ripped to bits, but his temper was quite good. After he'd told his tale I said to him "What are we going to do about it?" He said: "Oh, I don't know. 'Thank Heaven we have within the land five hundred as good as they.'"

Then he went off to report himself, and see if he could get on to the column that was going out in support. But not half an hour before I met him, I'd seen an agitated gentleman flogging a horse along the veldt and he had told me that the "flower of the British Army had been destroyed". Here were two men, under severe strain and excitement. One of them threw up a steadying quotation from the ancient, but quite modern, ballad of "Chevy Chase" and went on with his job. The other made bad worse by shouting what was nothing better than a news-paper, scare head-line; and, judging by the rate he was travelling, I don't think he reported for duty that night.

And that brings me to what I fear you will find more than usually dull.

I have spoken already of the advisability of a man knowing something about the classics. I have no Greek. Mine stopped at a little Greek Testament on Monday morning by gaslight before breakfast, and I depend for the rest of my knowledge on Bohn's cribs. But I got the ordinary allowance of Latin, ending with Virgil and

Horace—specially Horace. I don't pretend that I liked it, any more than I should have liked anything else that purported to be education, but looking back at it now, it strikes me as valuable. I believe in the importance of a man getting some classics ground into him in his youth even though, as far as his elders can see (but I don't think one's elders are quite the judges) there is no visible result. Men tell us that what we want nowadays is a modern and scientific education—something that will be of immediate use to a man in "the battle of life". They say that you could teach a child of twelve in a couple of terms as much Latin as the average public schoolboy carries away at the end of seven years; and the rest of the time could be devoted to studying modern languages and science and the things that are of immediate use to him. I haven't the least doubt you could. Any child of twelve could kodak any master-piece of Greek sculpture in less time than the cleverest artist in the world could begin to get ready to draw it. Any bright-minded intelligent pride of a prep.-school could in two terms learn the twenty or thirty odds and ends of quotations, the half-remembered Latin tags, which represent what the bulk of us carry away from our schools. I know a man who did much better than this.

He was a wonderful Greek scholar and at school and at college he took every scholarship and gold medal that was in sight, and before he was twenty-five he was appointed lecturer to his own College. Then he called on one of the dons who was a bit of a philosopher as well as a scholar. The old man asked him a few polite questions. Then he said: "You know Plato of course". My friend in a modest way said he thought he did. He had an idea at the back of his head that he knew Plato rather better than most men of his time. "Well," said the old man, "what's it all about?"

My friend scratched his head a little. Then it slowly dawned on him that he literally and absolutely did not know what Plato was all about. He knew pretty much everything else connected with the gentleman, but to put it roughly, what Plato was after, what Plato's game was in the world, my friend did not know. Then he sat down and began to think what Plato was all about. He's still thinking.

I have a notion that our intelligent child of twelve would be rather like my college friend without my friend's willingness to go back and think. He would know his quotations probably more accurately than we do for a while; but I doubt if he would know what they were about. They would not be part of his system, incorporated into him in seven years. They would not come back to him unconsciously, and most certainly their spirit would not.

I attach a certain amount of importance to the spirit of a few old Latin tags and quotations. Some of them, not more than three lines long, give one the very essence of what a man ought to try to do. Others, equally short, let you understand once and for all, the things that a man should not do—under any circumstances. There are others—bits of odes from Horace, they happen to be in my case—that make one realize in later life as no other words in any other tongue can, the brotherhood of mankind in time of sorrow or affliction. But men say that one can get the same stuff in an easier way and in a living tongue. They say there is no sense in dragging men up and down through grammar and construe for years and years, when at the last, all they can produce ("produce" is a good word) is a translation that would make Virgil, Horace or Cicero turn in their graves. Here is my defence of this alleged wicked waste of time. The reason why one has to parse and construe and grind at the dead tongues in which certain ideas are expressed, is not for, the sake of what is called intellectual training—that may be given in other ways—but because only in that tongue is that idea expressed with absolute perfection. If it were not so the Odes of Horace would not have survived. (People aren't in a conspiracy to keep things alive.) I grant you that the kind of translations one serves up at school are as bad and as bald as they can be. They are bound to be so, because one cannot re-express an idea that has been perfectly set forth. (Men tried to do this, by the way, in the revised version of the Bible. They failed.) Yet, by a painful and laborious acquaintance with the mechanism of that particular tongue; by being made to take it to pieces and put it together again, and by that means only; we can arrive at a state of mind in which, though we cannot re-express the idea in any adequate words, we can realize and feel and absorb the idea. To put it in this way. No one can play cricket like Ranji at his best. But to appreciate Ranji's play; to pick up enough from it to try and improve your own with; you must have played cricket for more than two terms.

Our ancestors were not fools. They knew what we, I think, are in danger of forgetting—that the whole background of life, in law, civil administration, conduct of life, the terms of justice, the terms of science, the value of government, are the everlasting ramparts of Rome and Greece—the father and mother of civilization. And for that reason, before they turned a man into life at large, they arranged that he should not merely pick up, but absorb into his system (through his hide if necessary) the fact that Greece and Rome were there. Later on, they knew, he would find out for himself how much and how important they were and they are, and that they still exist.

Some time ago I had the honour to meet a statesman who had been in charge of a great portion of the Empire. He was an old man, trained in the old school, and, talking about this very subject, he said something like this: "All I took away from school and college was the fact that there were once peoples who didn't talk our tongue and who were very strong on sacrifice and ritual, particularly at meals, whose gods were different from ours and who had strict views on the disposal of the dead. Well, you know, all that is worth knowing if you ever have to govern India."

I have never had to govern India, but I quite agree with him.

A certain knowledge of the classics is worth having, because it makes you realize that all the world is not like ourselves in all respects, and yet in matters that really touch the inside life of a man, neither the standards nor the game have changed.

I suppose I ought to apologize for the attitude I've taken. I certainly do apologize for taking so long to explain it. We will now revisit calmer scenes. Let me assure you for your comfort that Literature can't be taught, unless a man really wants to know something about it. Pieces or periods can be set and studied with notes, but that, thank goodness, is the worst that can happen.

One can't prescribe books, even the best books, to people unless one knows a good deal about each individual person. If a man is keen on reading, I think he ought to open his mind to some older man who knows him and his life, and to take his advice in the matter, and above all, to discuss with him the first books that interest him.

This idea applies only to what are called the standard authors—and—this is only my own theory. I don't know how it would work with you—the Elizabethan dramatists. You mustn't be afraid of fashions. The thing to remember is that all first-class stuff is as good and as new and as fresh now as in the day it was made.

But there are some things a man can't discuss with anyone, and it isn't right that he should. We have times and moods and tenses of black depression and despair and general mental discomfort which, for convenience sake, we call liver or sulks. But so far as my experience goes, that is just the time when a man is peculiarly accessible to the influence of a book, as he is to any other outside influence; and, moreover, that is just the time when he naturally and instinctively does not want anything of a mind-taxing soul-stirring nature. Then is the time to fall back on the books that, neither pretend to be nor are accepted as masterpieces, but books whose tone and temper soothe your trouble for the time being. A man who knows you and your life may be able to recommend such books. Ask him.

The thing to be careful of when you are in this mood is to come out of it as soon as it lifts, and not to continue dreaming over books because they suit that mood or because they minister to your own vanity. There have been a few great dreamers in the world who have achieved great things for the world; but for every dreamer whose dreams have been good, or at least not harmful, there are thousands who have been a hindrance to themselves, an expense to their families and a nuisance to mankind. Books used intemperately to excess become most dangerous drugs, and there is a type of book—modern I regret to say, as Mr. Pecksniff did not say about the Sirens—which is to be avoided when one's mind is a little off colour. One reads in a newspaper occasionally of the bold youth of ten who goes off with a knife and sevenpence halfpenny in coppers, to become a demon chauffeur or to lariat Red-Indians or shoot cowboys, and is then brought into court, weeping, by a policeman. And the magistrate says it's the sad result of reading—"Deadwood Dick or The Terror of Bloody Gulch". It's hard to realize that there is a mass of modern stuff which is practically no more than "Deadwood Dick" and the penny dreadful disguised and flavoured to modern taste. They fill the mind, they are meant to fill the mind, with a lot of vague and windy ideas that one can start off to do miracles or benefit one's fellow-men (which is the fashion just now), without training or equipment of any kind except a desire to astonish the world and show one's independence—exactly like the kid with the penknife and the stolen coppers. It is not probable that you'll come much in the way of these books, but if you do, before you read them, watch the men who discuss 'em and recommend 'em to you. If they strike you as the kind of men you'd like to be with in a tight place, or to go to if you were in trouble, then read them. Otherwise, as Sir Walter Raleigh said—"Otherwise not".

Most of you are going to enter what is called the life of action, in which you will discover that you will have to think harder, closer, and quicker than the bulk of men who take up what is so kindly called "the intellectual life". Harder, because you will be thinking against men, not books; closer, because your thoughts will be translated, several times a day perhaps, into action that may affect the lives and interests of men; quicker, because, even if you don't eventually make ghastly mistakes, you may have to alter your plans at a minute's notice to meet a changed situation. Incidentally, you will have to express your thoughts, wants, and orders both in speech and writing with much more clearness than the average literary man, and under circumstances that will not exactly lend themselves to clear thinking or easy writing. It is almost worse for a C.O. not to have expressive written (not spoken) words at his command than not to have men. With luck you can always scratch a few men together out of the hospitals or the Army Service Corps; but if you send in a report that nobody can make head or tail of, because you haven't the words to tell your case, you can lose a thousand men in half an hour. So you must get your words, and a working knowledge of the use of words. And words come out of literature—even if you make no other use of it.

Those of you who go into the Service will find out that, in spite of aeroplanes, you will have to guess, most of your time, at what is going on behind the next hill; and this is not only the whole business of war but of life. And those who have read *The Green Curve*, which is a splendid book, know that you will have to think what is in the mind of the man who is opposed to you. And you must do that in life as well as in the Service.

Well, half of Literature is placing fields that aren't there, and the rest of it is recording how every conceivable kind of ball that can be bowled by the Fates or life or circumstances has, at one time or another, been bowled at some wretched or happy man; and how he has played it. Life is too short to hunt up the individual record in each case; but, over and above all the help we can get from our ordinary training, association with our betters, and our very limited experience, we can pick up from Literature a few general and fundamental ideas as to how the great game of life has been played by the best players.

The man who writes for fools is always sure of a large audience ❡

On Books and Reading

Arthur Schopenhauer

Why do we read? How should we read? Is it bad to read too much? German philosopher and author of The World as Will and Representation *(one of Hitler's favourite texts) Arthur Schopenhauer (1788–1860) is known for his rather gloomy philosophical speculations and developing the theory of metaphysical voluntarism. He was not universally admired— Bertrand Russell said of him: "It is hard to find in his life evidences of any virtue except kindness to animals", but Leo Tolstoy was greatly impressed by him and Marilyn Monroe was interested enough in his opinions to own a copy of* The Philosophy of Schopenhauer *by Irwin Edman. Schopenhauer was certainly a keen reader and his mother Johanna was one of the most famous female authors in Germany at the start of the 19th century, running a hugely prestigious literary salon.*

In his essay "On Books and Reading" he is especially merciless on the effects of bad books—"those rank weeds of literature which extract nourishment from the corn and choke it"—and what not to read, as well as the value of re-reading. Schopen-hauer's own favourites were the ancient Sanskrit Upanishads and Baltasar Gracián's 17th century aphoristic The Art of Worldly Wisdom: A Pocket Oracle *which he translated from the original Spanish into German.*

Ignorance is degrading only when found in company with riches. The poor man is restrained by poverty and need: labour occupies his thoughts, and takes the place of knowledge. But rich men who are ignorant live for their lusts only, and are like the beasts of the field; as may be seen every day: and they can also be reproached for not having used wealth and leisure for that which gives them their greatest value.

When we read, another person thinks for us: we merely repeat his mental process. In learning to write, the pupil goes over with his pen what the teacher has outlined in pencil: so in reading; the greater part of the work of thought is already done for us. This is why it relieves us to take up a book after being occupied with our own thoughts. And in reading, the mind is, in fact, only the playground of another's thoughts. So it comes about that if anyone spends almost the whole day in reading, and by way of relaxation devotes the intervals to some thoughtless pastime, he gradually loses the capacity for thinking; just as the man who always rides, at last forgets how to walk. This is the case with many learned persons: they have read themselves stupid. For to occupy every spare moment in reading, and to do nothing but read, is even more paralyzing to the mind than constant manual labour, which at least allows those engaged in it to follow their own thoughts. A spring never free from the pressure of some foreign body at last loses its elasticity; and so does the mind if other people's thoughts are constantly forced upon it. Just as you can ruin the stomach and impair the whole body by taking too much nourishment, so you can overfill and choke the mind by feeding it too much. The more you read, the fewer are the traces left by what you have read: the mind becomes like a tablet crossed over and over with writing. There is no time for ruminating, and in no other way can you assimilate what you have read. If you read on and on without setting your own thoughts to work, what you have read cannot strike root, and is generally lost. It is, in fact, just the same with mental as with bodily food: hardly the fifth part of what one takes is assimilated. The rest passes off in evaporation, respiration and the like.

The result of all this is that thoughts put on paper are nothing more than footsteps in the sand: you see the way the man has gone, but to know what he saw on his walk, you want his eyes.

There is no quality of style that can be gained by reading writers who possess it; whether it be persuasiveness, imagination, the gift of drawing comparisons, boldness, bitterness, brevity, grace, ease of expression or wit, unexpected contrasts, a laconic or naive manner, and the like.

But if these qualities are already in us, exist, that is to say, potentially, we can call them forth and bring them to consciousness; we can learn the purposes to which they can be put; we can be strengthened in our inclination to use them, or get courage to do so; we can judge by examples the effect of applying them, and so acquire the correct use of them; and of course it is only when we have arrived at that point that we actually possess these qualities. The only way in which reading can form style is by teaching us the use to which we can put our own natural gifts. We must have these gifts before we begin to learn the use of them. Without them, reading teaches us nothing but cold, dead mannerisms and makes us shallow imitators.

The strata of the earth preserve in rows the creatures which lived in former ages; and the array of books on the shelves of a library stores up in like manner the errors of the past and the way in which they have been exposed. Like those creatures, they too were full of life in their time, and made a great deal of noise; but now they are stiff and fossilized, and an object of curiosity to the literary palaeontologist alone.

Herodotus relates that Xerxes wept at the sight of his army, which stretched further than the eye could reach, in the thought that of all these, after a hundred years, not one would be alive. And in looking over a huge catalogue of new books, one might weep at thinking that, when ten years have passed, not one of them will be heard of.

It is in literature as in life: wherever you turn, you stumble at once upon the incorrigible mob of humanity, swarming in all directions, crowding and soiling everything, like flies in summer. Hence the number, which no man can count, of bad books, those rank weeds of literature, which draw nourishment from the corn and choke it. The time, money and attention of the public, which rightfully belong to good books and their noble aims, they take for themselves: they are written for the mere purpose of making money or procuring places. So they are not only useless; they do positive mischief. Nine-tenths of the whole of our present literature has no other aim than to get a few shillings out of the pockets of the public; and to this end author, publisher and reviewer are in league.

Let me mention a crafty and wicked trick, albeit a profitable and successful one, practised by litterateurs, hack writers, and voluminous authors. In complete disregard of good taste and the true culture of the period, they have succeeded in getting the whole of the world of fashion into leading strings, so that they are all trained to read in time, and all the same thing, viz., *the newest books*; and that for the purpose of getting food for conversation in the circles in which they move. This is the aim served by bad novels, produced by writers who were once celebrated, as Spindler, Bulwer Lytton, Eugène Sue. What can be more miserable than the lot of a reading public like this, always bound to peruse the latest works of extremely commonplace persons who write for money only, and who are therefore never few in number? and for this advantage they are content to know by name only the works of the few superior minds of all ages and all countries. Literary newspapers, too, are a singularly cunning device for robbing the reading public of the time which, if culture is to be attained, should be devoted to the genuine productions of literature, instead of being occupied by the daily bungling commonplace persons.

Hence, in regard to reading, it is a very important thing to be able to refrain. Skill in doing so consists in not taking into one's hands any book merely because at the time it happens to be extensively read; such as political or religious pamphlets, novels, poetry, and the like, which make a noise, and may even attain to several editions in the first and last year of their existence. Consider, rather, that the man who writes for fools is always sure of a large audience; be careful to limit your time for reading, and devote it exclusively to the works of those great minds of all times and countries, who o'ertop the rest of humanity, those whom the voice of fame points to as such. These alone really educate and instruct. You can never read bad literature too little, nor good literature too much. Bad books are intellectual poison; they destroy the mind. Because people always read what is new instead of the best of all ages, writers remain in the narrow circle of the ideas which happen to prevail in their time; and so the period sinks deeper and deeper into its own mire.

There are at all times two literatures in progress, running side by side, but little known to each other; the one real, the other only apparent. The former grows into permanent literature; it is pursued by those who live *for* science or poetry; its course is sober and quiet, but extremely slow; and it produces in Europe scarcely a dozen works in a century; these, however, are permanent. The other kind is pursued by persons who live *on* science or poetry; it goes at a gallop with much noise and shouting of partisans; and every twelve-month puts a thousand works on the market. But after a few years one asks, Where are they? where is the glory which came so soon and made so much clamour? This kind may be called fleeting, and the other, permanent literature.

In the history of politics, half a century is always a considerable time; the matter which goes to form them is ever on the move; there is always something going on. But in the history of literature there is often a complete standstill for the same period; nothing has happened, for clumsy attempts don't count. You are just where you were fifty years previously.

To explain what I mean, let me compare the advance of knowledge among mankind to the course taken by a planet. The false paths on which humanity usually enters after every important advance are like the epicycles in the Ptolemaic system, and after passing through one of them, the world is just where it was before it entered it. But the great minds, who really bring the race further on its course do not accompany it on the epicycles it makes from time to time. This explains why posthumous fame is often bought at the expense of contemporary praise, and *vice versa*. An instance of such an epicycle is the philosophy started by Fichte and Schelling, and crowned by Hegel's caricature of it. This epicycle was a deviation from the limit to which philosophy had been ultimately brought by Kant; and at that point I took it up again afterwards, to carry it further. In the intervening period the sham philosophers I have mentioned and some others went through their epicycle, which had just come to an end; so that those who went with them on their course are conscious of the fact that they are exactly at the point from which they started.

This circumstance explains why it is that, every thirty years or so, science, literature, and art, as expressed in the spirit of the time, are declared bankrupt. The errors which appear from time to time amount to such a height in that period that the mere weight of their absurdity makes the fabric fall; whilst the opposition to them has been gathering force at the same time. So an upset takes place, often followed by an error in the opposite direction. To exhibit these movements in their periodical return would be the true practical aim of the history of literature: little attention, however, is paid to it. And besides, the comparatively short duration of these periods makes it difficult to collect the data of epochs long gone by, so that it is most convenient to observe how the matter stands in one's own generation. An instance of this tendency, drawn from physical science, is supplied in the Neptunian geology of Werner.

But let me keep strictly to the example cited above, the nearest we can take. In German philosophy, the brilliant epoch of Kant was immediately followed by a period which aimed rather at being imposing than at convincing. Instead of being thorough and clear, it tried to be dazzling, hyperbolical, and, in a special degree, unintelligible: instead of seeking truth, it intrigued. Philosophy could make no progress in this fashion; and at last the whole school and its method became bankrupt. For the effrontery of Hegel and his fellows came to such a pass—whether because they talked such sophisticated nonsense, or were so unscrupulously puffed, or because the entire aim of this pretty piece of work was quite obvious—that in the end there was nothing to prevent charlatanry of the whole business from becoming manifest to everybody: and when, in consequence of certain disclosures, the favour it had enjoyed in high quarters was withdrawn, the system was openly ridiculed. This most miserable of all the meagre philosophies that have ever existed came to grief, and dragged down with it into the abysm of discredit, the systems of Fichte and Schelling which had preceded it. And so, as far as Germany is concerned, the total philosophical incompetence of the first half of the century following upon Kant is quite plain: and still the Germans boast of their talent for philosophy in comparison with foreigners, especially since an English writer has been so maliciously ironical as to call them "a nation of thinkers."

For an example of the general system of epicycles drawn from the history of art, look at the school of sculpture which flourished in the last century and took its name from Bernini, more especially at the development of it which prevailed in France. The ideal of this school was not antique beauty, but commonplace nature: instead of the simplicity and grace of ancient art, it represented the manners of a French minuet.

This tendency became bankrupt when, under Winckelmann's direction, a return was made to the antique school. The history of painting furnishes an illustration in the first quarter of the century, when art was looked upon merely as a means and instrument of mediaeval religious sentiment, and its themes consequently drawn from ecclesiastical subjects alone: these, however, were treated by painters who had none of the true earnestness of faith, and in their delusion they followed Francesco Francia, Pietro Perugino, Angelico da Fiesole and others like them, rating them higher even than the really great masters who followed. It was in view of this terror, and because in poetry an analogous aim had at the same time found favour, that Goethe wrote his parable *Pfaffenspiel*. This school, too, got the reputation of being whimsical, became bankrupt, and was followed by a return to nature, which proclaimed itself in *genre* pictures and scenes of life of every kind, even though it now and then strayed into what was vulgar.

The progress of the human mind in literature is similar. The history of literature is for the most part like the catalogue of a museum of deformities; the spirit in which they keep best is pigskin. The few creatures that have been born in goodly shape need not be looked for there. They are still alive, and are everywhere to be met with in the world, immortal, and with their years ever green. They alone form what I have called real literature; the history of which, poor as it is in persons, we learn from our youth up out of the mouths of all educated people, before compilations recount it for us.

As an antidote to the prevailing monomania for reading literary histories, in order to be able to chatter about everything, without having any real knowledge at all, let me refer to a passage in Lichtenberg's works (vol. II., p. 302), which is well worth perusal.

I believe that the over-minute acquaintance with the history of science and learning, which is such a prevalent feature of our day, is very prejudicial to the advance of knowledge itself. There is pleasure in following up this history; but as a matter of fact, it leaves the mind, not empty indeed, but without any power of its own, just because it makes it so full. Whoever has felt the desire, not to fill up his mind, but to strengthen it, to develop his faculties and aptitudes, and generally, to enlarge his powers, will have found that there is nothing so weakening as intercourse with a so-called litterateur, on a matter of knowledge on which he has not thought at all, though he knows a thousand little facts appertaining to its history and literature. It is like reading a cookery-book when you are hungry. I believe that so-called literary history will never thrive amongst thoughtful people, who are conscious of their own worth and the worth of real knowledge. These people are more given to employing their own reason than to troubling themselves to know how others have employed theirs. The worst of it is that, as you will find, the more knowledge takes the direction of literary research, the less the power of promoting knowledge becomes; the only thing that increases is pride in the possession of it. Such persons believe that they possess knowledge in a greater degree than those who really possess it. It is surely a well-founded remark, that knowledge never makes its possessor proud. Those alone let themselves be blown out with pride, who incapable of extending knowledge in their own persons, occupy themselves with clearing up dark points in its history, or are able to recount what others have done. They are proud, because they consider this occupation, which is mostly of a mechanical nature, the practice of knowledge.

I could illustrate what I mean by examples, but it would be an odious task.

Still, I wish someone would attempt a *tragical* history of literature, giving the way in which the writers and artists, who form the proudest possession of the various nations which have given them birth, have been treated by them during their lives. Such a history would exhibit the ceaseless warfare, which what was good and genuine in all times and countries has had to wage with what was bad and perverse. It would tell of the martyrdom of almost all those who truly enlightened humanity, of almost all the great masters of every kind of art: it would show us how, with few exceptions, they were tormented to death, without recognition, without sympathy, without followers; how they lived in poverty and misery, whilst fame, honour, and riches, were the lot of the unworthy; how their fate was that of Esau, who while he was hunting and getting venison for his father, was robbed of the blessing by Jacob, disguised in his brother's clothes, how, in spite of all, they were kept up by the love of their work, until at last the bitter fight of the teacher of humanity is over, until the immortal laurel is held out to him, and the hour strikes when it can be said:

Der schwere Panzer wird zum Fluegelkleide
Kurz ist der Schmerz, unendlich ist die Freude.

The heavy armour becomes the winged dress
brief is the pain, unending is the joy.

No book ought to be squeezed or even coaxed into its place ❡

On Books and the Housing of Them

W.E. Gladstone

Keen reader, book collector, and Prime Minister, William Ewart Gladstone (1809–1898) was also so preoccupied with the importance of bookshelves and libraries that he wrote a ground-breaking booklet about them in 1890. It is now very scarce and Anne Fadiman writes about her surprise in coming across a copy in a bookshop in her book about books Ex Libris. *"If you wish to understand the character of W.E. Gladstone and Victorian England," she writes, "everything you need to know is contained within the small compass of 'On Books and the Housing of Them'." Gladstone is said to have always had a book with him wherever he went and according to his own estimates read more than 20,000, adding his own marginalia to around half these volumes. "In a room well filled with them [books]," he writes in the essay below, "no one has felt or can feel solitary".*

Gladstone started collecting during his schoolboy days at Eton, continued as a student at Oxford, and throughout his life enjoyed visiting bookshops. By 1889, he had amassed such a collection that he decided to found his eponymous library in Hawarden, Wales, Britain's only Prime Ministerial library and which is also now a hotel. Gladstone endowed it with £40,000 and more than 30,000 of his own books, many of which he personally transported from his home to the library by wheelbarrow. "What man," he wrote, "who really loves his books delegates to any other human being, as long as there is breath in his body, the office of introducing them into their homes?" Today, it holds more than 200,000 covering all subjects, including much of Gladstone's own correspondence.

In the old age of his intellect (which at this point seemed to taste a little of decrepitude), Strauss declared that the doctrine of immortality has recently lost the assistance of a passable argument, inasmuch as it has been discovered that the stars are inhabited; for where, he asks, could room now be found for such a multitude of souls? Again, in view of the current estimates of prospective population for this earth, some people have begun to entertain alarm for the probable condition of England (if not Great Britain) when she gets (say) seventy millions that are allotted to her against six or eight hundred millions for the United States. We have heard in some systems of the pressure of population upon food; but the idea of any pressure from any quarter upon space is hardly yet familiar. Still, I suppose that many a reader must have been struck with the naive simplicity of the hyperbole of St. John, perhaps a solitary unit of its kind in the New Testament: "the which if they should be written every one, I suppose that even the world itself could not contain the books that should be written."

A book, even Audubon (I believe the biggest known), is smaller than a man; but, in relation to space, I entertain more proximate apprehension of pressure upon available space from the book population than from the numbers of mankind. We ought to recollect, with more of a realized conception than we commonly attain to, that a book consists, like a man, from whom it draws its lineage, of a body and a soul. They are not always proportionate to each other. Nay, even the different members of the book-body do not sing, but clash, when bindings of a profuse costliness are imposed, as too often happens in the case of Bibles and books of devotion, upon letter-press which is respectable journeyman's work and nothing more. The men of the Renascence had a truer sense of adaptation; the age of jewelled bindings was also the age of illumination and of the beautiful *miniatura*, which at an earlier stage meant side or margin art, and then, on account of the small portraitures included in it, gradually slid into the modern sense of miniature. There is a caution which we ought to carry with us more and more as we get in view of the coming period of open book trade, and of demand practically boundless. Noble works ought not to be printed in mean and worthless forms, and cheapness ought to be limited by an instinctive sense and law of fitness. The binding of a book is the dress with which it walks out into the world. The paper, type and ink are the body, in which its soul is domiciled. And these three, soul, body, and habiliment, are a triad which ought to be adjusted to one another by the laws of harmony and good sense.

Already the increase of books is passing into geometrical progression. And this is not a little remarkable when we bear in mind that in Great Britain, of which I speak, while there is a vast supply of cheap works, what are termed "new publications" issue from the press, for the most part, at prices fabulously high, so that the class of real purchasers has been extirpated, leaving behind as buyers only a few individuals who might almost be counted on the fingers, while the effective circulation depends upon middle-men through the engine of circulating libraries. These are not so much owners as distributors of books, and they mitigate the difficulty of dearness by subdividing the cost, and then selling such copies as are still in decent condition at a large reduction. It is this state of things, due, in my opinion, principally to the present form of the law of copyright, which perhaps may have helped to make way for the satirical (and sometimes untrue) remark that in times of distress or pressure men make their first economies on their charities, and their second on their books.

The annual arrivals at the Bodleian Library are, I believe, some twenty thousand; at the British Museum, forty thousand, sheets of all kinds included. Supposing three-fourths of these to be volumes, of one size or another, and to require on the average an inch of shelf space, the result will be that in every two years nearly a mile of new shelving will be required to meet the wants of a single library. But, whatever may be the present rate of growth, it is small in comparison with what it is likely to become. The key of the question lies in the hands of the United Kingdom and the United States jointly. In this matter there rests upon these two Powers no small responsibility. They, with their vast range of inhabited territory, and their unity of tongue, are masters of the world, which will have to do as they do. When the Britains and America are fused into one book market; when it is recognized that letters, which as to their material and their aim are a high-soaring profession, as to their mere remuneration are a trade; when artificial fetters are relaxed, and printers, publishers, and authors obtain the reward which well-regulated commerce would afford them, then let floors beware lest they crack, and walls lest they bulge and burst, from the weight of books they will have to carry and to confine.

It is plain, for one thing, that under the new state of things specialism, in the future, must more and more abound. But specialism means subdivision of labour; and with subdivision labour ought to be more completely, more exactly, performed. Let us bow our heads to the inevitable; the day of encyclopaedic learning has gone by. It may perhaps be said that that sun set with Leibnitz. But as little learning is only dangerous when it forgets that it is little, so specialism is only dangerous when it forgets that it is special. When it encroaches on its betters, when it claims exceptional certainty or honour, it is impertinent, and should be rebuked; but it has its own honour in its own province, and is, in any case, to be preferred to pretentious and flaunting sciolism.

A vast, even a bewildering prospect is before us, for evil or for good; but for good, unless it be our own fault, far more than for evil. Books require no eulogy from me; none could be permitted me, when they already draw their testimonials from Cicero and Macaulay. But books are the voices of the dead. They are a main instrument of communion with the vast human procession of the other world. They are the allies of the thought of man. They are in a certain sense at enmity with the world. Their work is, at least, in the two higher compartments of our threefold life. In a room well filled with them, no one has felt or can feel solitary. Second to none, as friends to the individual, they are first and foremost among the compages, the bonds and rivets of the race, onward from that time when they were first written on the tablets of

Babylonia and Assyria, the rocks of Asia minor, and the monuments of Egypt, down to the diamond editions of Mr. Pickering and Mr. Frowde.

It is in truth difficult to assign dimensions for the libraries of the future. And it is also a little touching to look back upon those of the past. As the history of bodies cannot, in the long run, be separated from the history of souls, I make no apology for saying a few words on the libraries which once were, but which have passed away.

The time may be approaching when we shall be able to estimate the quantity of book knowledge stored in the repositories of those empires which we call prehistoric. For the present, no clear estimate even of the great Alexandrian Libraries has been brought within the circle of popular knowledge; but it seems pretty clear that the books they contained were reckoned, at least in the aggregate, by hundreds of thousands. The form of the book, however, has gone through many variations; and we moderns have a great advantage in the shape which the exterior has now taken. It speaks to us symbolically by the title on its back, as the roll of parchment could hardly do. It is established that in Roman times the bad institution of slavery ministered to a system under which books were multiplied by simultaneous copying in a room where a single person read aloud in the hearing of many the volume to be reproduced, and that so produced they were relatively cheap. Had they not been so, they would hardly have been, as Horace represents them, among the habitual spoils of the grocer. It is sad, and is suggestive of many inquiries, that this abundance was followed, at least in the West, by a famine of more than a thousand years. And it is hard, even after all allowances, to conceive that of all the many manuscripts of Homer which Italy must have possessed we do not know that a single parchment or papyrus was ever read by a single individual, even in a convent, or even by a giant such as Dante, or as Thomas Aquinas, the first of them unquestionably master of all the knowledge that was within the compass of his age. There were, however, libraries even in the West, formed by Charlemagne and by others after him. We are told that Alcuin, in writing to the great monarch, spoke with longing of the relative wealth of England in these precious estates. Mr. Edwards, whom I have already quoted, mentions Charles the Fifth of France, in 1365, as a collector of manuscripts. But some ten years back the Director of the Bibliothèque Nationale informed me that the French King John collected twelve hundred manuscripts, at that time an enormous library, out of which several scores were among the treasures in his care. Mary of Medicis appears to have amassed in the sixteenth century, probably with far less effort, 5,800 volumes. Oxford had before that time received noble gifts for her University Library. And we have to recollect with shame and indignation that that institution was plundered and destroyed by the Commissioners of the boy King Edward the Sixth, acting in the name of the Reformation of Religion. Thus it happened that opportunity was left to a private individual, the munificent Sir Thomas Bodley, to attach an individual name to one of the famous libraries of the world. It is interesting to learn that municipal bodies have a share in the honour due to monasteries and sovereigns in the collection of books; for the Common Council of Aix purchased books for a public library in 1419.

Louis the Fourteenth, of evil memory, has at least this one good deed to his credit, that he raised the Royal Library at Paris, founded two centuries before, to 70,000 volumes. In 1791 it had 150,000 volumes. It profited largely by the Revolution. The British Museum had only reached 115,000 when Panizzi became keeper in 1837. Nineteen years afterward he left it with 560,000, a number which must now have more than doubled. By his noble design for occupying the central quadrangle, a desert of gravel until his time, he provided additional room for 1,200,000 volumes. All this apparently enormous space for development is being eaten up with fearful rapidity; and such is the greed of the splendid library that it opens its jaws like Hades, and threatens shortly to expel the antiquities from the building, and appropriate the places they adorn.

But the proper office of hasty retrospect in a paper like this is only to enlarge by degrees, like the pupil of an eye, the reader's contemplation and estimate of the coming time, and to prepare him for some practical suggestions of a very humble kind. So I take up again the thread of my brief discourse. National libraries draw upon a purse which is bottomless. But all public libraries are not national. And the case even of private libraries is becoming, nay, has become, very serious for all who are possessed by the inexorable spirit of collection, but whose ardour is perplexed and qualified, or even baffled, by considerations springing from the balance-sheet.

The purchase of a book is commonly supposed to end, even for the most scrupulous customer, with the payment of the bookseller's bill. But this is a mere popular superstition. Such payment is not the last, but the first term in a series of goodly length. If we wish to give to the block a lease of life equal to that of the pages, the first condition is that it should be bound. So at least one would have said half a century ago. But, while books are in the most instances cheaper, binding, from causes which I do not understand, is dearer, at least in England, than it was in my early years, so that few can afford it. We have, however, the tolerable and very useful expedient of cloth binding (now in some danger, I fear, of losing its modesty through flaring ornamentation) to console us. Well, then, bound or not, the book must of necessity be put into a bookcase. And the bookcase must be housed. And the house must be kept. And the library must be dusted, must be arranged, should be catalogued. What a vista of toil, yet not unhappy toil! Unless indeed things are to be as they now are in at least one princely mansion of this country, where books, in thousands upon thousands, are jumbled together with no more arrangement than a sack of coals; where not even the sisterhood of consecutive volumes has been respected; where undoubtedly an intending reader may at the mercy of Fortune take something from the shelves that is a book; but where no particular book can, except by the purest accident, be found.

Such being the outlook, what are we to do with our books? Shall we be buried under them like Tarpeia under the Sabine shields? Shall we renounce them (many will, or will do worse, will keep to the most worthless part of them) in our resentment against their more and more exacting demands? Shall we sell and scatter them? as it is painful to see how often the books of eminent men are ruthlessly, or at least unhappily, dispersed on their decease. Without answering in detail, I shall assume that the book-buyer is a book-lover, that his love is a tenacious, not a transitory love, and that for him the question is how best to keep his books.

I pass over those conditions which are the most obvious, that the building should be sound and dry, the apartment airy, and with abundant light. And I dispose with a passing anathema of all such as would endeavour to solve their problem, or at any rate compromise their difficulties, by setting one row of books in front of another. I also freely admit that what we have before us is not a choice between difficulty and no difficulty, but a choice among difficulties.

The objects further to be contemplated in the bestowal of our books, so far as I recollect, are three: economy, good arrangement, and accessibility with the smallest possible expenditure of time.

In a private library, where the service of books is commonly to be performed by the person desiring to use them, they ought to be assorted and distributed according to subject. The case may be altogether different where they have to be sent for and brought by an attendant. It is an immense advantage to bring the eye in aid of the mind; to see within a limited compass all the works that are accessible, in a given library, on a given subject; and to have the power of dealing with them collectively at a given spot, instead of hunting them up through an entire accumulation. It must be admitted, however, that distribution by subjects ought in some degree to be controlled by sizes. If everything on a given subject, from folio down to 32mo, is to be brought locally together, there will be an immense waste of space in the attempt to lodge objects of such different sizes in one and the same bookcase. And this waste of space will cripple us in the most serious manner, as will be seen with regard to the conditions of economy and of accessibility. The three conditions are in truth all connected together, but especially the two last named.

Even in a paper such as this the question of classification cannot altogether be overlooked; but it is one more easy to open than to close—one upon which I am not bold enough to hope for uniformity of opinion and of practice. I set aside on the one hand the case of great public libraries, which I leave to the experts of those establishments. And, at the other end of the scale, in small private libraries the matter becomes easy or even insignificant. In libraries of the medium scale, not too vast for some amount of personal survey, some would multiply subdivision, and some restrain it. An acute friend asks me under what and how many general headings subjects should be classified in a library intended for practical use and reading, and boldly answers by suggesting five classes only: (1) science, (2) speculation, (3) art, (4) history, and (5) miscellaneous and periodical literature. But this seemingly simple division at once raises questions both of practical and of theoretic difficulty. As to the last, periodical literature is fast attaining to such magnitude, that it may require a classification of its own, and that the enumeration which indexes supply, useful as it is, will not suffice. And I fear it is the destiny of periodicals as such to carry down with them a large proportion of what, in the phraseology of railways, would be called dead weight, as compared with live weight. The limits of speculation would be most difficult to draw. The diversities included under science would be so vast as at once to make sub-classification a necessity. The -ologies are by no means well suited to rub shoulders together; and sciences must include arts, which are but country cousins to them, or a new compartment must be established for their accommodation. Once more, how to cope with the everlasting difficulty of "Works"? In what category to place Dante, Petrarch, Swedenborg, Burke, Coleridge, Carlyle, or a hundred more? Where, again, is Poetry to stand? I apprehend that it must take its place, the first place without doubt, in Art; for while it is separated from Painting and her other "sphere-born harmonious sisters" by their greater dependence on material forms they are all more inwardly and profoundly united in their first and all-enfolding principle, which is to organize the beautiful for presentation to the perceptions of man.

But underneath all particular criticism of this or that method of classification will be found to lie a subtler question—whether the arrangement of a library ought not in some degree to correspond with and represent the mind of the man who forms it. For my own part, I plead guilty, within certain limits, of favouritism in classification. I am sensible that sympathy and its reverse have something to do with determining in what company a book shall stand. And further, does there not enter into the matter a principle of humanity to the authors themselves? Ought we not to place them, so far as may be, in the neighbourhood which they would like? Their living manhoods are printed in their works. Every reality, every tendency, endures. *Eadem sequitur tellure sepultos.*[1]

I fear that arrangement, to be good, must be troublesome. Subjects are traversed by promiscuous assemblages of "works;" both by sizes; and all by languages. On the

[1] "The same follows them to their rest"

whole I conclude as follows. The mechanical perfection of a library requires an alphabetical catalogue of the whole. But under the shadow of this catalogue let there be as many living integers as possible, for every well-chosen subdivision is a living integer and makes the library more and more an organism. Among others I plead for individual men as centres of subdivision: not only for Homer, Dante, Shakespeare, but for Johnson, Scott, and Burns, and whatever represents a large and manifold humanity.

The question of economy, for those who from necessity or choice consider it at all, is a very serious one. It has been a fashion to make bookcases highly ornamental. Now books want for and in themselves no ornament at all. They are themselves the ornament. Just as shops need no ornament, and no one will think of or care for any structural ornament, if the goods are tastefully disposed in the shop-window. The man who looks for society in his books will readily perceive that, in proportion as the face of his bookcase is occupied by ornament, he loses that society; and conversely, the more that face approximates to a sheet of bookbacks, the more of that society he will enjoy. And so it is that three great advantages come hand in hand, and, as will be seen, reach their maximum together: the sociability of books, minimum of cost in providing for them, and ease of access to them.

In order to attain these advantages, two conditions are fundamental. First, the shelves must, as a rule, be fixed; secondly, the cases, or a large part of them, should have their side against the wall, and thus, projecting into the room for a convenient distance, they should be of twice the depth needed for a single line of books, and should hold two lines, one facing each way. Twelve inches is a fair and liberal depth for two rows of octavos. The books are thus thrown into stalls, but stalls after the manner of a stable, or of an old-fashioned coffee-room; not after the manner of a bookstall, which, as times go, is no stall at all, but simply a flat space made by putting some scraps of boarding together, and covering them with books.

This method of dividing the longitudinal space by projections at right angles to it, if not very frequently used, has long been known. A great example of it is to be found in the noble library of Trinity College, Cambridge, and is the work of Sir Christopher Wren. He has kept these cases down to very moderate height, for he doubtless took into account that great heights require long ladders, and that the fetching and use of these greatly add to the time consumed in getting or in replacing a book. On the other hand, the upper spaces of the walls are sacrificed, whereas in Dublin, All Souls, and many other libraries the bookcases ascend very high, and magnificent apartments walled with books may in this way be constructed. Access may be had to the upper portions by galleries; but we cannot have stairs all round the room, and even with one gallery of books a room should not be more than from sixteen to eighteen feet high if we are to act on the principle of bringing the largest possible number of volumes into the smallest possible space. I am afraid it must be admitted that we cannot have a noble and imposing spectacle, in a vast apartment, without sacrificing economy and accessibility; and vice versa.

The projections should each have attached to them what I rudely term an endpiece (for want of a better name), that is, a shallow and extremely light adhering bookcase (light by reason of the shortness of the shelves), which both increases the accommodation, and makes one short side as well as the two long ones of the parallelepiped to present simply a face of books with the lines of shelf, like threads, running between the rows.

The wall-spaces between the projections ought also to be turned to account for shallow bookcases, so far as they are not occupied by windows. If the width of the interval be two feet six, about sixteen inches of this may be given to shallow cases placed against the wall.

Economy of space is in my view best attained by fixed shelves. This dictum I will now endeavour to make good.

If the shelves are movable, each shelf imposes a dead weight on the structure of the bookcase, without doing anything to support it. Hence it must be built with wood of considerable mass, and the more considerable the mass of wood the greater are both the space occupied and the ornament needed. When the shelf is fixed, it contributes as a fastening to hold the parts of the bookcase together; and a very long experience enables me to say that shelves of from half- to three-quarters of an inch worked fast into uprights of from three-quarters to a full inch will amply suffice for all sizes of books except large and heavy folios, which would probably require a small, and only a small, addition of thickness.

I have recommended that as a rule the shelves be fixed, and have given reasons for the adoption of such a rule. I do not know whether it will receive the sanction of authorities. And I make two admissions. First, it requires that each person owning and arranging a library should have a pretty accurate general knowledge of the sizes of his books. Secondly, it may be expedient to introduce here and there, by way of exception, a single movable shelf; and this, I believe, will be found to afford a margin sufficient to meet occasional imperfections in the computation of sizes. Subject to these remarks, I have considerable confidence in the recommendation I have made.

I will now exhibit to my reader the practical effect of such arrangement, in bringing great numbers of books within easy reach. Let each projection be three feet long, twelve inches deep (ample for two faces of octavos), and nine feet high, so that the upper shelf can be reached by the aid of a wooden stool of two steps not more than twenty inches high, and portable without the least effort in a single hand. I will suppose the wall space available to be eight feet, and the projections, three in number, with end pieces need only jut out three feet five, while narrow strips of bookcase will run up the wall between the projections. Under these conditions, the bookcases thus described will carry above 2,000 octavo volumes.

And a library forty feet long and twenty feet broad, amply lighted, having some portion of the centre fitted with very low bookcases suited to serve for some of the uses of tables, will receive on the floor from 18,000 to 20,000 volumes of all sizes, without losing the appearance of a room or assuming that of a warehouse, and while leaving portions of space available near the windows for purposes of study. If a gallery be added, there will be accommodation for a further number of five thousand, and the room need be no more than sixteen feet high. But a gallery is not suitable for works above the octavo size, on account of inconvenience in carriage to and fro.

It has been admitted that in order to secure the vital purpose of compression with fixed shelving, the rule of arrangement according to subjects must be traversed partially by division into sizes. This division, however, need not, as to the bulk of the library, be more than threefold. The main part would be for octavos. This is becoming more and more the classical or normal size; so that nowadays the octavo edition is professionally called the library edition. Then there should be deeper cases for quarto and folio, and shallower for books below octavo, each appropriately divided into shelves.

If the economy of time by compression is great, so is the economy of cost. I think it reasonable to take the charge of provision for books in a gentleman's house, and in the ordinary manner, at a shilling a volume. This may vary either way, but it moderately represents, I think, my own experience, in London residences, of the charge of fitting up with bookcases, which, if of any considerable size, are often unsuitable for removal. The cost of the method which I have adopted later in life, and have here endeavoured to explain, need not exceed one penny per volume. Each bookcase when filled represents, unless in exceptional cases, nearly a solid mass. The intervals are so small that, as a rule, they admit a very small portion of dust. If they are at a tolerable distance from the fireplace, if carpeting be avoided except as to small movable carpets easily removed for beating, and if sweeping be discreetly conducted, dust may, at any rate in the country, be made to approach to a *quantité négligeable*.

It is a great matter, in addition to other advantages, to avoid the endless trouble and the miscarriages of movable shelves; the looseness, and the tightness, the weary arms, the aching fingers, and the broken fingernails. But it will be fairly asked what is to be done, when the shelves are fixed, with volumes too large to go into them? I admit that the dilemma, when it occurs, is formidable. I admit also that no book ought to be squeezed or even coaxed into its place: they should move easily both in and out. And I repeat here that the plan I have recommended requires a pretty exact knowledge by measurement of the sizes of books and the proportions in which the several sizes will demand accommodation. The shelf-spacing must be reckoned beforehand, with a good deal of care and no little time. But I can say from experience that by moderate care and use this knowledge can be attained, and that the resulting difficulties, when measured against the aggregate of convenience, are really insignificant. It will be noticed that my remarks are on minute details, and that they savour more of serious handiwork in the placing of books than of lordly survey and direction. But what man who really loves his books delegates to any other human being, as long as there is breath in his body, the office of inducting them into their homes?

And now as to results. It is something to say that in this way 10,000 volumes can be placed within a room of quite ordinary size, all visible, all within easy reach, and without destroying the character of the apartment as a room. But, on the strength of a case with which I am acquainted, I will even be a little more particular. I take as before a room of forty feet in length and twenty in breadth, thoroughly lighted by four windows on each side; as high as you please, but with only about nine feet of height taken for the bookcases: inasmuch as all heavy ladders, all *adminicula* requiring more than one hand to carry with care, are forsworn. And there is no gallery. In the manner I have described, there may be placed on the floor of such a room, without converting it from a room into a warehouse, bookcases capable of receiving, in round numbers, 20,000 volumes.

The state of the case, however, considered as a whole, and especially with reference to libraries exceeding say 20,000 or 30,000 volumes, and gathering rapid accretions, has been found to require in extreme cases, such as those of the British Museum and the Bodleian (on its limited site), a change more revolutionary in its departure from, almost reversal of, the ancient methods, than what has been here described.

The best description I can give of its essential aim, so far as I have seen the processes (which were tentative and initial), is this. The masses represented by filled bookcases are set one in front of another; and, in order that access may be had as it is required, they are set upon trams inserted in the floor (which must be a strong one), and wheeled off and on as occasion requires.

The idea of the society of books is in a case of this kind abandoned. But even on this there is something to say. Neither all men nor all books are equally sociable. For my part I find but little sociability in a huge wall of *Hansards*, or (though a great improvement) in the *Gentleman's Magazine*, in the *Annual Registers*, in the *Edinburgh* and *Quarterly Reviews*, or in the vast range of volumes which represent pamphlets innumerable. Yet each of these and other like items variously present to us the admissible, or the valuable, or the indispensable. Clearly these masses, and such as these, ought to be selected first for what I will not scruple to call interment. It is a burial; one, however, to which the process of cremation will never of set purpose be applied. The word I have used is dreadful, but also dreadful is the thing. To have our dear old friends stowed away in catacombs, or like the wine-bottles in bins: the simile is surely lawful until the use of that commodity shall have been prohibited by the growing movement of the time. But however we may gild the case by a cheering illustration, or by the remembrance that the provision is one called for only by our excess of wealth, it can hardly be contemplated without a shudder at a process so repulsive applied to the best beloved among inanimate objects.

It may be thought that the gloomy perspective I am now opening exists for great public libraries alone. But public libraries are multiplying fast, and private libraries are aspiring to the public dimensions. It may be hoped that for a long time to come no grave difficulties will arise in regard to private libraries, meant for the ordinary use of that great majority of readers who read only for recreation or for general improvement. But when study, research, authorship, come into view, when the history of thought and of inquiry in each of its branches, or in any considerable number of them, has to be presented, the necessities of the case are terribly widened. Chess is a specialty and a narrow one. But I recollect a statement in the *Quarterly Review*, years back, that there might be formed a library of twelve hundred volumes upon chess. I think my deceased friend, Mr. Alfred Denison, collected between two and three thousand upon angling. Of living Englishmen perhaps Lord Acton is the most effective and retentive reader; and for his own purposes he has gathered a library of not less, I believe, than 100,000 volumes.

Undoubtedly the idea of book-cemeteries such as I have supposed is very formidable. It should be kept within the limits of the dire necessity which has evoked it from the underworld into the haunts of living men. But it will have to be faced, and faced perhaps oftener than might be supposed. And the artist needed for the constructions it requires will not be so much a librarian as a warehouseman.

But if we are to have cemeteries, they ought to receive as many bodies as possible. The condemned will live ordinarily in pitch darkness, yet so that when wanted, they may be called into the light. Asking myself how this can most effectively be done, I have arrived at the conclusion that nearly two-thirds, or say three-fifths, of the whole cubic contents of a properly constructed apartment may be made a nearly solid mass of books: a vast economy which, so far as it is applied, would probably quadruple or quintuple the efficiency of our repositories as to contents, and prevent the population of Great Britain from being extruded some centuries hence into the surrounding waters by the exorbitant dimensions of their own libraries.

Some books are to be tasted, others to be swallowed ❡

Of Studies

Francis Bacon

Francis Bacon (1561–1626) was the very definition of a Renaissance man; a philosopher, diplomat, member of Parliament (for several constituencies), occultist (with possible Rosicrucian and Freemasonry links), scientist (who developed the scientific method in his treatise "Novum Organum", 1620), writer (even, some would argue, of Shakespeare's plays), and lawyer. He was also keen on libraries and put together a classification system using three categories—philosophy, history and poesy—which each had sub-categories.

Bacon is also widely considered to be the first major essayist and his "Essaies: Religious Meditations. Places of Perswasion and Disswasion. Seene and Allowed" (1597) focuses on a wide range of subjects from gardens to boldness as well as this short piece below in which he wisely comments that "Reading maketh a full man" (and woman, of course).

His career was rather a rollercoaster—not one of Elizabeth I's avowed favourites, Bacon prospered under her successor James I until he was brought down by a bribery scandal that effectively ended his public life. In his Brief Lives *biography, John Aubrey recounts that Bacon died after developing pneumonia from an experiment involving stuffing a chicken with ice. He was buried at St Michael's Church in St Albans, Hertfordshire, near his home of Gorhambury.*

Studies serve for delight, for ornament, and for ability. Their chief use for delight, is in privateness and retiring; for ornament, is in discourse; and for ability, is in the judgment, and disposition of business. For expert men can execute, and perhaps judge of particulars, one by one; but the general counsels, and the plots and marshalling of affairs, come best, from those that are learned. To spend too much time in studies is sloth; to use them too much for ornament, is affectation; to make judgment wholly by their rules, is the humour of a scholar. They perfect nature, and are perfected by experience: for natural abilities are like natural plants, that need pruning, by study; and studies themselves, do give forth directions too much at large, except they be bounded in by experience. Crafty men condemn studies, simple men admire them, and wise men use them; for they teach not their own use; but that is a wisdom without them, and above them, won by observation. Read not to contradict and confute; nor to believe and take for granted; nor to find talk and discourse; but to weigh and consider. Some books are to be tasted, others to be swallowed, and some few to be chewed and digested; that is, some books are to be read only in parts; others to be read, but not curiously; and some few to be read wholly, and with diligence and attention. Some books also may be read by deputy, and extracts made of them by others; but that would be only in the less important arguments, and the meaner sort of books, else distilled books are like common distilled waters, flashy things. Reading maketh a full man; conference a ready man; and writing an exact man. And therefore, if a man write little, he had need have a great memory; if he confer little, he had need have a present wit: and if he read little, he had need have much cunning, to seem to know, that he doth not. Histories make men wise; poets witty; the mathematics subtle; natural philosophy deep; moral grave; logic and rhetoric able to contend. *Abeunt studia in mores*[1]. Nay, there is no stond or impediment in the wit, but may be wrought out by fit studies; like as diseases of the body, may have appropriate exercises. Bowling is good for the stone and reins; shooting for the lungs and breast; gentle walking for the stomach; riding for the head; and the like. So if a man's wit be wandering, let him study the mathematics; for in demonstrations, if his wit be called away never so little, he must begin again. If his wit be not apt to distinguish or find differences, let him study the Schoolmen; for they are *cymini sectores*[2]. If he be not apt to beat over matters,

1 "Studies pass into and influence manners"
2 "Splitters of hairs"

and to call up one thing to prove and illustrate another, let him study the lawyers' cases. So every defect of the mind, may have a special receipt.

They may not have as many lives as a cat, but they certainly die hard ⁊

On Destroying Books

J.C. Squire

Magazine editor, poet, and journalist, Sir John Collings Squire is best known today not for his sterling work editing the New Statesman *and literary magazine the* London Mercury, *but as the inspiration for one of the finest pieces of comic writing about sport. Squire (1884–1958) was a leading light of the early 20th century Georgian movement of poets and was the centre of a Bloomsbury-type literary group known as the Squirearchy. As "William Hodge", the captain of a motley cricket team in A.G. Macdonell's gently satirical* England, Their England *(1933), he plays a central role in the famous cricket match episode (and in a less flattering light appears as "Jack Spire" in Evelyn Waugh's* Decline and Fall*). The wandering cricket team Squire established, The Invalids, which was the inspiration for Hodge's side, is still going strong today.*

Indeed, there were many strings to Squire's bow. In 1922 he adapted Pride and Prejudice *for the stage starring Ellen Terry, and two years later was one of the distinguished contributors to the royal mini-library of Queen Mary's Dolls' House (he wrote a special acrostic sonnet). The phrase "I am not so think as you drunk I am" is attributed to him and he was also very keen on Stilton cheese, suggesting a public monument to its creator be erected.*

In the column below, Squire begins by considering the worth of the books donated to soldiers during the First World War before moving on to the problems of disposing of unwanted volumes. It was one of his pieces for his regular humorous "Books in General" column in the New Statesman, *a collection of which was published in 1919 under the pseudonym Solomon Eagle, including essays on "Other People's Books" and "Moving a Library".*

It says in the paper that over two million volumes have been presented to the troops by the public. It would be interesting to inspect them. Most of them, no doubt, are quite ordinary and suitable; but it was publicly stated the other day that some people were sending the oddest things, such as magazines twenty years old, guides to the Lake District, Bradshaws, and back numbers of *Whitaker's Almanack*. In some cases, one imagines, such indigestibles get into the parcels by accident; but it is likely that there are those who jump at the opportunity of getting rid of books they don't want. Why have they kept them if they don't want them? But most people, especially non-bookish people, are very reluctant to throw away anything that looks like a book. In the most illiterate houses that one knows every worthless or ephemeral volume that is bought finds its way to a shelf and stays there. In reality it is not merely absurd to keep rubbish merely because it is printed: it is positively a public duty to destroy it. Destruction not merely makes more room for new books and saves one's heirs the trouble of sorting out the rubbish or storing it: it may also prevent posterity from making a fool of itself. We may be sure that if we do not burn, sink, or blast all the superseded editions of Bradshaw, two hundred years hence some collector will be specializing in old railway time-tables, gathering, at immense cost, a complete series, and ultimately leaving his "treasures" (as the Press will call them) to a Public Institution.

But it is not always easy to destroy books. They may not have as many lives as a cat, but they certainly die hard; and it is sometimes difficult to find a scaffold for them. This difficulty once brought me almost within the Shadow of the Rope. I was living in a small and (as Shakespeare would say) heaven-kissing flat in Chelsea, and books of inferior minor verse gradually accumulated there until at last I was faced with the alternative of either evicting the books or else leaving them in sole, undisturbed tenancy and taking rooms elsewhere for myself. Now, no one would have bought these books. I therefore had to throw them away or wipe them off the map altogether. But how? There were scores of them. I had no kitchen range, and I could not toast them on the gas-cooker or consume them leaf by leaf in my small study fire—for it is almost as hopeless to try to burn a book without opening it as to try to burn a piece of granite. I had no dust-bin; my debris went down a kind of flue behind the staircase, with small trap-doors opening to the landings. The difficulty with this was that the larger books might choke it; the authorities, in fact, had labelled it "Dust and Ashes Only"; and in any case I did not want to leave the books intact, and some dustman's unfortunate family to get a false idea of English poetry from them. So in the end I determined to do to them what so many people do to the kittens: tie them up and consign them to the river. I improvised a sack, stuffed the books into it, put it over my shoulder, and went down the stairs into the darkness.

It was nearly midnight as I stepped into the street. There was a cold nip in the air; the sky was full of stars; and the greenish-yellow lamps threw long gleams across the smooth, hard road. Few people were about; under the trees at the corner a Guardsman was bidding a robust goodnight to his girl, and here and there rang out the steps of solitary travellers making their way home across the bridge to Battersea. I turned up my overcoat collar, settled my sack comfortably across my shoulders, and strode off towards the little square glow of the coffee-stall which marked the near end of the bridge, whose sweeping iron girders were just visible against the dark sky behind. A few doors down I passed a policeman who was flashing his lantern on the catches of basement windows. He turned. I fancied he looked suspicious, and I trembled slightly. The thought occurred to me: "Perhaps he suspects I have swag in this sack." I was not seriously disturbed, as I knew that I could bear investigation, and that nobody would be suspected of having stolen such goods (though they were all first editions) as I was carrying. Nevertheless I could not help the slight unease which comes to all who are eyed suspiciously by the police, and to all who are detected in any deliberately furtive act, however harmless. He acquitted me, apparently; and, with a step that, making an effort, I prevented from growing more rapid, I walked on until I reached the Embankment.

It was then that all the implications of my act revealed themselves. I leaned against the parapet and looked down into the faintly luminous swirls of the river. Suddenly I heard a step near me; quite automatically I sprang back from the wall and began walking on with, I fervently hoped, an air of rumination and unconcern. The pedestrian came by me without looking at me. I was a tramp, who had other things to think about; and, calling myself an ass, I stopped again. "Now's for it," I thought; but just as I was preparing to cast my books upon the waters I heard another step—a slow and measured one. The next thought came like a blaze of terrible blue lightning across my brain: "What about the splash?" A man leaning at midnight over the Embankment wall: a sudden fling of his arms: a great splash in the water. Surely, and not without reason, whoever was within sight and hearing (and there always seemed to be someone near) would at once rush to me and seize me. In all probability they would think it was a baby. What on earth would be the good of telling a London constable that I had come out into the cold and stolen down alone to the river to get rid of a pack of poetry? I could almost hear his gruff, sneering laugh: "You tell that to the Marines, my son!"

So, for I do not know how long I strayed up and down, increasingly fearful of being watched, summoning up my courage to take the plunge and quailing from it at the last moment. At last I did it. In the middle of Chelsea Bridge there are projecting circular bays with seats in them. In an agony of decision I left the Embankment and hastened straight for the first of these. When I reached it I knelt on the seat. Looking over, I hesitated again. But I had reached the turning-point. "What!" I thought savagely, "under the resolute mask that you show your friends is there really a shrinking and contemptible coward? If you fail now, you must never hold your head up again. Anyhow, what if you are hanged for it? Good God! You worm, better men than you have gone to the gallows!" With the courage of despair I took a heave. The sack dropped sheer. A vast splash. Then silence fell again. No one came. I turned home; and as I walked I thought a little sadly of all those books falling into that old torrent, settling slowly down through the pitchy dark, and subsiding at last on the ooze of the bottom, there to lie forlorn and forgotten whilst the unconscious world of men went on.

Horrible bad books, poor innocent books, you are lying there still; covered, perhaps, with mud by this time, with only a stray rag of your sacking sticking out of the slime into the opaque brown tides. Odes to Diana, Sonnets to Ethel, Dramas on the Love of Lancelot, Stanzas on a First Glimpse of Venice, you lie there in a living death, and your fate is perhaps worse than you deserved. I was harsh with you. I am sorry I did it. But even if I had kept you, I will certainly say this: I should not have sent you to the soldiers.

ALEX JOHNSON

A BOOK OF BOOK LISTS

EVERY BOOK ART GARFUNKEL HAS READ SINCE 1968
The Dead Poets Society Poems
A PRIME MINISTER'S BOOKSHELF
OSCAR WILDE'S READING GAOL BOOKCASE
CHARLES DARWIN'S TO READ LIST
DAVID BOWIE'S 100 INFLUENCERS
BOOKS LEFT BEHIND IN HOTELS
BURNT BY THE NAZIS
ALL THE PRESIDENTS' BOOKS
QUEEN MARY'S DOLLS' HOUSE LIBRARY
THE WRATH OF KHAN: A STAR TREK BOOKSHELF
Marilyn Monroe's Private Library
MPs' Most Borrowed Books
THE BOOKS ON THE INTERNATIONAL SPACE STATION
Desert Island Discs: The books
Scott's *Discovery* Library
SCOTTISH PRISONERS' FAVOURITE BOOKS
THE WORLD'S UNIVERSITIES' READING LISTS
BOOKS THAT HAVE NEVER BEEN WRITTEN
MOST CHALLENGED BOOKS IN AMERICA
MOST POPULAR OUT-OF-PRINT BOOKS
BANNED BOOKS AT GUANTÁNAMO DETAINEE LIBRARY
BOOKS IKEA USES AS DECORATION IN ITS SHOPS
LOST BOOKS
BOOKS 'WRITTEN' BY SHERLOCK HOLMES
THE UK'S TOP 20 REVISITED READS
THE FAKE BOOKS OF CHARLES DICKENS
BIN LADEN'S BOOKSHELF
RICHARD III'S LIBRARY

THE BRITISH LIBRARY

Also available from Alex Johnson